6·95

COMPUTERS AND LITERACY

Open University Press

English, Language, and Education series

General Editor: Anthony Adams

Lecturer in Education, University of Cambridge

This series is concerned with all aspects of language in education from the primary school to the tertiary sector. Its authors are experienced educators who examine both principles and practice of English subject teaching and language across the curriculum in the context of current educational and societal developments.

TITLES IN THE SERIES

Computers and Literacy
   Daniel Chandler and Stephen Marcus (eds.)
Children Talk About Books: Seeing Themselves as Readers
   Donald Fry
The English Department in a Changing World
   Richard Knott

In preparation

English Teaching: Programmes and Policies
   Anthony Adams and Esmor Jones
Microcomputers and the Language Arts
   Brent Robinson
Teaching Literature for Examinations
   Robert Protherough

COMPUTERS AND LITERACY

Edited by

Daniel Chandler and Stephen Marcus

Open University Press

Milton Keynes · Philadelphia

Open University Press
12 Cofferidge Close
Stony Stratford
Milton Keynes MK11 1BY, England
and
242 Cherry Street
Philadelphia, PA 19106, USA

First Published 1985

British Library Cataloguing in Publication Data
Computers and literacy. — (English language and
   education series)
   1. English language — Study and teaching —
   Computer assisted instruction
   I. Chandler, Daniel   II. Marcus, Stephen
   III. Series
   420'.7'8   PE1066

ISBN 0–335–15031–4

Library of Congress Cataloging in Publication Data
Main entry under title:
Computers and literacy.
   Bibliography:p.
   Includes Indexes.
   1.   Computers and literacy — Congresses.   2.   English
language — Study and teaching — Data processing —
Congresses.   3.   Language arts — Data Processing — Congresses.
I.   Chandler, Daniel.   II.   Marcus, Stephen.
LC149.5.C65   1985   428'.0028'5   85-3109

ISBN 0–335–15031–4

Typeset by S & S Press, Abingdon, Oxfordshire
Printed in Great Britain by St. Edmundsbury Press, Bury St. Edmunds,
Suffolk.

Contents

List of contributors

Anthony Adams is a lecturer at the Department of Education in the University of Cambridge, England. Over the past few years he has spoken on the theme of computers and the language arts throughout Britain and North America. His most recent book (with Esmor Jones) was *Teaching Humanities in the Microelectronic Age* (Open University Press, 1983).

Daniel Chandler, formerly an English teacher, is now co-partner (with David Butler) in Imagineering, a program design consultancy based in Llanybydder, Wales. He is the author of three books and many articles on computers in education: his most recent book was *Young Learners and the Microcomputer* (Open University Press, 1984) and his programs include FACTFILE (Cambridge University Press, 1982) and, with David Butler, ABC and TALKBACK (Acornsoft, 1984).

Michael Clark is deputy head at Heaton Manor School in Newcastle upon Tyne in England. He has been responsible for several projects involving the use of the Microwriter (a British hand-held word-processor) with young children, and gave presentations on this theme at both the 1983 and 1984 NATE commissions on computers in the language arts.

Dr David Dillon is based at the Department of Elementary Education at the University of Alberta in Canada. He is currently editor of the journal *Language Arts*. He gave one of the main presentations at the International Commission on Computers and Literacy in April 1984, his lecture forming the basis for his chapter in this book.

Dr Stephen Marcus is Associate Director of the South Coast Writing Project at the University of California in Santa Barbara. He is a contributing editor for the journal *Computers, Reading and Language Arts* and has written many articles on computers in education. Well-known throughout the United States for his interest in the use of computers as a writing tool, his program COMPUPOEM is an aid for drafting poetry.

Brent Robinson, formerly head of English at Westgate School in Winchester, is now based at the Department of Education at the University of Cambridge, England. The author of many articles and a forthcoming book on computers and the language arts, he has a special interest in the effect of computer-assisted activities on group discussion and the exploration of appropriate reading strategies for computer-based media.

Diana Thomson is well-known in England for her tireless work on behalf of MUSE (Microcomputer Users in Education), an organization established by teachers interested in the whole range of computer applications. Together with Christopher Pointeer she gave a presentation at the commission on computers and literacy at the University of Durham.

Edward Versluis is a member of the English Faculty at Southern Oregon State College. Together with Charles Ryberg he has given many presentations on the theme of computers in English and the language arts, and has been responsible for the development of several Apple-based programs, including PENGUINS OF DEATH and AUNT SADIE'S GIFT.

General Editor's Introduction

This book, with its many contributors from both sides of the Atlantic, is itself a product of the technology of which it speaks. Virtually all its chapters were drafted using microcomputers and the text was exchanged between authors and editors on disc, making it possible to amend them in the light of editorial comment with the minimum of time delay.

Daniel Chandler speaks in his introductory chapter of the changing nature of publication in the microelectronics age and several of the contributors clearly have this in mind in their comments on the future of the printed word. There is no doubt that our definition of literacy is changing rapidly as a consequence of the new technology, and this volume is a timely one in the light of contemporary developments.

The use of computer technology for the writing of the book has also made possible its rapid production following the 1984 conference of the National Association for the Teaching of English (NATE), out of which it grew. One of the features of this conference was a large and international commission on microcomputers and English teaching which Daniel Chandler chaired. Each of the contributors to the present volume took part in this commission and it is largely in consequence that the transatlantic dialogue represented in the book became possible. We are especially glad to be able to introduce to UK readers the work of Chandler's co-editor, Dr Stephen Marcus, of the University of California at Santa Barbara. Dr Marcus will need less introduction to readers in North America for he is one of the editors of an influential journal, *Computers, Reading and Language Arts.* It is a particular pleasure for me to be able to introduce Dr Marcus to a British public since I was privileged to be a member of a workshop that he conducted in 1983 on word-processing as part of the proceedings of the annual convention of the National Council for Teachers of English (NCTE). I was much impressed not only by his good sense and good humour but also by the skill with which he introduced a large and very varied audience to the techniques he was describing, involving them all, very quickly, in a variety of 'hands-on' experiences. Along with Chandler I was instrumental in persuading Marcus to come to England for the 1984 NATE Conference, and this book is the richer both for his editing and his own contributions.

Amongst the other North American contributors who were at the 1984 conference was David Dillon, editor of NCTE's journal *Language Arts*, who teaches in Canada at the University of Alberta. Several commission members were also present from Australia and New Zealand. The importance of this meeting of persons from the English-speaking world cannot be over-stressed. One of the most important contributions that computers are already making to the future of literacy is the shrinking of the world of communications. As I write these words, a promotional leaflet has arrived through my letter-box inviting me to become a subscriber to Knowledge Index which promises a 'vast instant reference library' and Dialmail, an 'electronic mail service giving access to thousands of people around the world'. All this can be accessed through my home microcomputer in combination with a modem and telephone line making it possible for me to communicate from my own home with mainframe computers around the world. A glance at any contemporary computing magazine will show how much this is the way things are currently developing in the microcomputing world. Electronic mail is becoming something that we are taking more and more for granted as part of our everyday lives. The evidence is very clear that the impact of microelectronics and computing generally will make more rather than fewer demands upon literacy, and that the definition of literacy will have to be extended to include screen reading and writing if it is to be adequate to the needs of those growing up in present-day society.

This will need to be recognized in schools, of course, but also in the home. With the growing penetration of computers into the home the demands of reading and writing have increased there also. This is why the intention of the present volume is to address interested parents as well as those involved in formal education. Several of the contributors, especially Daniel Chandler, have stressed the way in which education and learning as a product of the 'networked society' is rapidly breaking its traditional boundaries. For a number of reasons, of which the microcomputer is only one, we are likely to move towards a new conception of lifelong learning and towards the processes of community education. It has clearly been the intention of the editors and contributors to this volume to address themselves to these issues as well as to those of the more formal educational system.

Given its title, the book has necessarily concentrated upon the future of reading and writing in the microelectronic age, though the concerns of talking and listening have not been forgotten and are dealt with throughout, not only in the chapter explicitly concerned with oracy. But Daniel Chandler's opening chapter and the work of David Dillon and Stephen Marcus remind us that we must not take for granted a too optimistic and starry-eyed view of the future. Like all technologies the microcomputer can be used for good or ill, and it is important for us to play a conscious part in shaping the future that will result from the easy availability of this new and powerful tool of communication.

Although it is primarily addressed to educators, the present volume is one that should concern us all as citizens also. It is one of a series of books from the Open University Press which seek to open a debate on wider cultural issues that go beyond the bounds of the school-room alone.

Anthony Adams

Words of Thanks

This book arises out of the International Commission on Computers and Literacy held at the University of Durham in April 1984 and chaired by Daniel Chandler. This was part of the annual conference of the National Association for the Teaching of English (NATE). The commission provided a rare opportunity for a sharing of ideas between classroom teachers (both primary and secondary), lecturers in English and Education, and software designers and developers from both sides of the Atlantic. We would like to thank the Chair of NATE, Gordon Hodgeon, and the conference organizers, especially Pat Barrett, Margaret Bond and Peter Harris, for making the event possible.

We thank also all the members of the commission for giving so much of their time and themselves. Since these numbered over a hundred we are unable to list them, but we can at least express our warm appreciation for the hard work of those who helped with the administration: especially Phil Moore, Rosslyn Nelson and Marion Watts. Joe Telford and Maurice Edmundson kindly provided a great deal of computer equipment. Apart from sessions run by the contributors to this book, other commission sessions were run by: Betsy Barber, Carl Billson, Jan Bright, David Butler, Richard Ennals, James Gilman, Tony Gray, George Keith, Dr Gloria Kuchinskas, Professor Ronald LaConte, Majorie Pappas, Chris Pointeer, Charles Ryberg, Christopher Schenk, Dr Mike Sharples, Drs Irene and Owen Thomas, and Don Walton. Many of these presentations fed ideas into the discussions which were chaired by the contributors to this book; reflections on some of the themes appear in their chapters.

The editors would also like to record their special thanks to those who have read and commented on drafts of some of the sections in this book: Rose Chandler, Don Clark, Phil Moore, Mike Sharples, Irene Thomas and Edward Versluis.

Daniel Chandler
Stephen Marcus
November 1984

1 Computers and Literacy

DANIEL CHANDLER

T: You really ought to use this thing. Once you've picked it up you can stop worrying about not being able to remember things: it does it for you! You'd be amazed at the clever things you can do with it: you'll discover talents you didn't realize you had. And you'll realize how wise you were to try it.

A: It's a fascinating invention. But I'm afraid I've never believed that those who sell an idea are the best judges of its worth. People who use this thing will become dependent on it and soon they'll stop thinking altogether. I know that there'll be lots of people who'll say that anyone who can use it is brilliant, but just owning a way of storing vast amounts of information doesn't make you clever, does it? Will people know how to use it – that's the question? And what kind of world would it be if everyone was dependent on this kind of thing?

S: Exactly. You can't really learn anything from using it: all it can do is tell us what we already know.

P: Quite right.

S: At least if you ask a person something you've a fair chance of having a useful conversation. If we have to use this thing there'll be only one answer to each question, regardless of who asks it and whether they understand the answer. And what about people who abuse the system: how could we protect the information we put into it?

P: I couldn't agree more.

How many times have we heard that kind of conversation? An enthusiast who has just discovered computing tries to convey the excitement to a group of friends who haven't exactly caught the bug. After all, the device which has been largely responsible for the spread of popular awareness of computing – the microcomputer – only appeared in the US in 1975, reaching Britain three years later. But the source of this conversation predates the microcomputer. Indeed, it even precedes the mainframe computer (ENIAC appeared in 1946). What then, were these people talking about, and when?

It is only fair to admit that the passage has been paraphrased to disguise its origin, but although the referent has been obscured, the substance of the text is much the same. What might the subjects be? It's clearly some kind of technology. There's a concern that it will make us feeble-minded, and some may be tempted to suggest that it might be television. But the invention in question came far earlier than that.

In fact one of the critics was a teacher, and the conversation was recorded nearly two and a half thousand years ago – by Plato, in the *Phaedrus*. And the technology which Socrates perceived as such a threat to teaching and learning (indeed to the entire framework of the oral culture of classical Greece) was the technology of writing and reading. You, the reader, are in his terms a technocrat.

Literacy as a technology

Although the irony is, of course, that if Plato had not written the words we would not be able to read them now, the purpose of referring to his discussion of the issue is not to dismiss his concerns. Firstly, in the context of the split between the 'two cultures' in modern industrialized societies it may be a helpful corrective to perceive literacy as a technology. Secondly, in many ways, Plato was right. The spread of writing and reading did have profound effects. Writing and printing have transformed not only our culture but also the very nature of our consciousness[1] (indeed it is the fact that the technology of literacy has become so deeply interiorized that makes it so difficult for us to regard it as a technology).

Harold Innis has shown how changes in communications technology alter the way we think, what we think about, and the nature of community.[2] Whilst new media don't necessarily banish earlier ones (writing obviously didn't replace talking), they can come to dominate our cultural priorities (story-telling is now virtually a lost art). Literacy certainly led to a radical transformation of the nature of formal education. Whilst writing is clearly a potentially powerful tool (particularly in the exploration of abstract ideas), one of the major criticisms which can be levelled at contemporary schools is that they have indeed become obsessed with writing (though often purely as a ritualistic indication of learning), and they grossly undervalue the importance of talk to the learner. In this context Plato might well have agreed with Oscar Wilde's remark that literacy destroyed communication (precisely the same fears that many of us have about the computer).

Like writing, print has not been only a liberating influence in our culture. Of course, print on paper allows us to share, study and build on ideas in ways which are not open to oral cultures. But with the printing press came the concept that ideas have 'authors' and may even be 'owned' by them, that authors are special and set apart, and that books have 'authority' in validating ideas. And schools are places where one may still commonly find rooms full of children silently and passively reading 'texts' and where, in many cases, the educational priorities ('the Basics') are purely technological, revolving around the transmission of conventions for the expression of ideas dictated by the printed word.

It may be interesting to reflect on some of the characteristics of the mediation of ideas in the eras of script and print, and in this context to speculate about how a 'networked society'[3] might compare with script and print cultures.

MS and early print culture	The spread of literacy	Networked society
Books rare	Books widespread	Books special
Authorship not important	Rise of author	Decline of author: writing more collaborative
Clerics as distributors	Rise of publishers	Writers as publishers
Changeable texts	Definitive texts	Changeable texts
Copying important	Concept of plagiarism	Death of copyright
Authority	Individualism	Communality
Reading aloud/ listening	Private, silent reading	Participatory reading
Varied orthography	Writing conventions	Challenge to conventions of writing
International (Latin)	National	International

The arrival of computers won't of itself result in any change in the way in which technologies are used. There is nothing inevitable about the direction of change, and technologies cannot be divorced from the social and political context in which they are used. As Frank Smith has pointed out, there is at the same time the possibility that computers could destroy literacy by being used as narrowly instructional devices and an alternative direction in which we could use them as creative tools which might extend the power of literacy. Computers build on literacy, and even the voice-controlled computers of the future cannot alter the fundamental nature of all technologies of literacy as systems for manipulating symbols. Just like writing and print, computers bring with them both restrictive and liberating possibilities. But like the pen and the book, the computer is a tool, and provided that we are aware of the strengths and weaknesses of this medium, like any other, we can decide whether its use is appropriate for particular purposes, and how we will use it.

Changing the character and context of literacy

In one sense, computers have nothing to do with English and the Language Arts. They were not designed for 'educational' applications, still less for schools, and certainly not with narrowly curricular objectives in mind. Given the sad history of language laboratories and mechanical 'teaching machines' in Britain this is just as well. Computers are general-purpose intellectual tools, far more widely available outside schools than inside them, and perhaps with wider implications for what and how we learn than whatever we do in schools in the name of extending literacy. Given the backgrounds of the contributors and the likely audience for this kind of book it is hardly surprising that the contributors have chosen to address themselves almost exclusively to applications within schools, but as an editorial aside I would like to stress that as computers spread in domestic environments it will become essential to consider this dimension. As language-driven tools they are likely to have far wider effects on literacy than television, although what these effects will be is still a matter for speculation.

There seems little doubt that computers can make writing far more accessible to children. As I have written elsewhere,[4] many young children report that they find the word-processor a far easier tool to handle than the pen, and their efforts are, of course, rewarded with very presentable results. Text produced using a word-processor can look as good as the text in a printed book, and this is an important factor in reducing the gap which children perceive between their own writing and the printed book. The editing facilities of word-processors also offer a far more supportive environment for drafting than pen and paper, and can encourage children to improve the content as well as the appearance of their writing (although some observers have suggested that children may concentrate on low-level editing even with word-processors).[5]

Writing with a word-processor also seems to encourage writers to come closer to looking at their texts as readers. It is of course only when children come to regard writing as serving a real purpose – being addressed to readers who genuinely want to read what they have written – that they discover its power. When access to national and even international networks becomes more common in schools, libraries and the home, writers will also have easy access to vast audiences (acting as their own publishers), rather than the limited and artificial audiences which are still the norm for most writing in schools. Networks can also offer opportunities for an immediate response to writing, which, once again, is rare in schools. And such systems will offer children the rare opportunity not to be defined by age, allowing their writing to be read for its own worth. I recently heard of an American college professor who was enthusiastically corresponding with another user of a network who seemed to be very knowledgeable on some topic they were both concerned with, until the professor asked the other user what his job was. When he discovered that the user was a child, his enthusiasm evaporated and he ended the communication.

Seymour Papert has provocatively suggested that the regular availability of computers in domestic environments could lead children to write almost as soon as they learn to talk, and if Papert's vision were to become a widespread reality, we would be forced to re-read the writings of deschoolers such as Ivan Illich as somewhat more than an academic exercise. Certainly there is evidence that some pre-school children with regular access to computers are able to learn to write competently (though these children are invariably operating in extraordinarily supportive home environments).[6] Increasing numbers of children will no doubt begin their schooling already able to use a keyboard but unable to write with a pen. If schools do not adapt to meet their needs – if they do not grasp the new opportunities the medium offers – it may prove the last straw for the growing number of parents who are feeling alienated by the inadequacies of schooling.

The image of technology in literature

We have been bombarded with powerful negative images of technology in mainstream literature for over two hundred years. William Blake's 'dark, satanic mills' have mistakenly become for many a potent image of industrial technology. Mary Shelley's gothic novel, *Frankenstein* (1818), dramatizes a powerful feeling that our technological creations may one day turn on us, and Isaac Asimov has coined the term 'the Frankenstein complex' to describe the common fear of such a phenomenon. In *Hard Times* (1854), Dickens shows factory discipline dominating not only work but also (through an application of the metaphor of the machine) school and human relationships in general.

In Samuel Butler's *Erewhon* (1872) the Frankenstein theme is extended when a philosopher argues that machines will eventually develop a complex consciousness and will then control humankind. The narrator argues that, even now, 'Man's very soul is due to the machines; it is a machine-made thing; he thinks as he thinks, and feels as he feels, through the work that his machines have wrought upon him, and their existence is quite as much a *sine qua non* for his, as for theirs . . .'.[7]

E. M. Forster's story, 'The Machine Stops' (1928), portrays a world cut off completely from nature. People live in compartments sealed off from one another and all forms of interaction are mediated through the machine: 'There were buttons and switches everywhere — buttons to call for food, for music, for clothing . . . There was the button that produced literature. And there were of course the buttons by which she communicated with her friends'. The very idea of direct experience has become terrifying.

Aldous Huxley's *Brave New World* appeared in 1932. The main focus here is on achieving a stable society: complete social control is accomplished through genetic programming and conditioning. The novel reflects an anxiety that the evolution of our machine-based civilization has become an autonomous process. George Orwell's even bleaker dystopian novel, *Nineteen Eighty-Four*, was written sixteen years later. In his novel, of course, technology is used for surveillance, for the destruction of the evidence of history, for torture and mass murder. Orwell voiced more subtle concerns in *The Road to Wigan Pier* when he observed that 'like a drug, the machine is useful, dangerous and habit-forming', and 'so long as the machine is there, one is under an obligation to use it'.

The influence of such writers on teachers in the Humanities has no doubt been a major factor in the evolution of their feelings about technology. In Britain, the views of the critic F. R. Leavis (himself influenced by D. H. Lawrence's criticisms of industrial society) have also had a major influence on the attitudes of several generations of English teachers in the schools towards modern technology in general (and the mass media in particular). In their influential book, *Culture and Environment* (1933), Leavis and Denys Thompson wrote that: 'The great agent of change, and, from our point of view, destruction, has of course been the machine – applied power. The machine has brought us many advantages, but it has destroyed the old ways of life, the old forms, and by reason of the continual rapid change it involves, prevented the growth of new'.[8]

Surely Plato would have shared their feelings when they observed that: 'In the old rural England speech was an art . . . Instead of reading newspapers or going to the cinema or turning on the loudspeaker on the gramophone people talked; talked at work and at rest, at the public house, at market, by the wayside and at the cottage door.[9] Leavis and Thompson did not suggest trying to turn back the clock. They wrote that 'It is useless to think in terms of emulating the Erewhonians and scrapping the machine in the hope of restoring the old order. Even if agriculture were revived, that would not bring back the organic community'. Their strategy was 'to insist on what has been lost lest it should be forgotten; for the memory of the old order must be the chief incitement towards a new, if ever we are to have one. If we forget the old order we shall not know what kind of thing to strive towards, and in the end there will be no striving, but a surrender to the "progress" of the machine'.[10]

Although without doubt the mainstream literature of our industrial era has been full of negative images of technology, perhaps it is worth reminding ourselves that there are alternative strands in literature. The poetry of Donne and Milton is suffused with the inspiration derived from the use of the latest technological developments: microscopes and telescopes. Despite Jonathan Swift's criticisms of the applications of technology in the Academy at Lagado we should not overlook the fact that he makes effective use of the device of magnifying anatomical details in Brobdingnag. And as a notable exception to the preoccupations of nineteenth-century writers, William Morris's *News from Nowhere* (1890) does not exhibit a purely dystopian stance towards technology: 'All work which would be irksome to do by hand is done by immensely improved machinery; and in all work which it is a pleasure to do by hand machinery is done without'.[11]

In Britain at least the legacy of literature and Leavis has been a 'civil defence' strategy by English teachers anxious to protect children from the evils of modern industrial society (in particular, the mass media). For such teachers the computer is often just another invasive influence in the classroom. It will no doubt be many years before there is any general shift in this stance. Without doubt there is a need for critical stances towards technology, especially in education, but if these are to involve a complete rejection of any technology, teachers would deserve to be regarded as failing to cope with the full range of children's needs. Above all, to survive in a society characterized by change we need to be able to adapt to it rather than simply retreat from it. Writers such as Donne, Milton and Morris, without suspending their critical faculties, were excited by some of the possibilities of change. Justly mindful of the dangers of the biases of new communications media, teachers involved in the language arts today cannot afford to neglect the excitement of a technology which will undoubtedly have major implications for literacy.

Will computers restrict children's language?

A common question from English teachers on in-service courses in Britain is whether using computers will restrict rather than extend children's language development. It is, of course, an important question to ask. Although various research studies suggest that using computers frequently seems to stimulate rather than restrict the spoken language of children when used in the context of collaborative activities,[12] much of the current software both in Britain and the US allows only a very limited use of written language. Even in the future the kinds of written language we can use both in programs and in programming will always be far less rich than the full range of written language we are all capable of using.

Confronted by particular pieces of software, however, perhaps we need to bear in mind that it may be that using computers will simply encourage different kinds of language for different purposes, and that no computer program is an isolated learning experience – it is important to see it in context (for example, the context teachers provide in the classroom). Of course, if all learning were to be mediated through computers it would inevitably have a reductionist influence on language. But so would the use of books or television in this way. If the computer is only one of a number of media to which children are exposed (as will always be the case outside school, even if any specific medium is rejected by them) then it can only broaden their experience of different kinds of language in different contexts. If teachers completely reject computers on these grounds they may be neglecting to support children in appropriate uses of major kinds of language which it will certainly be necessary to employ in some contexts outside school.

Using computers involves not only a different kind of use of language but also a different kind of thinking. Whether or not one accepts Papert's argument that simply using computers allows us to become conscious of the very notion of different styles of thinking,[13] the medium often demands a very precise and systematic thinking style. And whether or not one agrees with Papert about the particular value of such a style it is a mode of thinking which is relatively unfamiliar in schools and which it is uniquely capable of supporting.

The value of the computer may be in supporting this style of thinking as one of a number of tools which each have particular advantages and disadvantages for particular purposes. If our concern is to support children in developing a mastery of language in all its modes we may decide that what children may need to learn is how to choose and use appropriate media for specific purposes.

The danger always remains, of course, that the kind of language and thinking which we employ with computers could be accorded far too much importance as against other modes. In society at large there are already signs that the computer may be contributing to a Hobbesian equation of reasoning with reckoning in popular debate. Because computers make reckoning easier it is tempting to apply it to contexts where it may not always be appropriate. Values and feelings can never be encapsulated in formulae, and any use of computers which may lead us to underestimate or even ignore individuals and to think merely in terms of numbers must surely be resisted. In society at large there is already the danger that the use of computers by central and local government as a tool of policy-making can lead to the adoption of purely utilitarian strategies. In schools, a case in point is a very popular 'resource management' game variously known as EMPIRE or HAMMURABI. In the context of such games it is not uncommon to hear such casual remarks as: 'We did rather well this season – only 500 people died'.

Simulations incorporating models of behaviour could also encourage children to adopt dangerously simplistic and mechanistic social or biological metaphors. Any use of electronic databases should always involve an awareness of the selective nature of the data available, the limitations of the classification system and the kinds of questions which it allows the user to ask, and the accuracy and completeness of the 'answers' provided. The use of both simulations and electronic 'information' systems can divorce data from more direct experience, and such mediation must not automatically be regarded as a substitute. Nor should these electronic systems be regarded as necessarily more appropriate than other techniques in educational applications – dramatic role-play is likely to be of more value than purely computer-based simulation in exploring human feelings about social issues (though there is no reason why the two techniques shouldn't be used together). Using printed sources may be far more useful than using an electronic encyclopedia if you want to browse or compare one page with another.

An easy answer to the question of whether language-driven programs may restrict the language of young users is that the capability of such software to handle natural language is increasing all the time. The implication is that we will eventually be able to interact with computers in language far closer to our own ordinary everyday language (even using speech rather than the keyboard). Apart from the objection that this has not yet happened, there is a more serious concern which we may need to consider. This is that however sophisticated the language-handling capabilities of computers may become, they will never truly 'understand' us, and yet the expansion of these capabilities may delude us into thinking that they do. As Joseph Weizenbaum showed with his program ELIZA, even simple 'conversational' programs seem able to convince some people that they are dealing with some kind of intelligence. There is already cause for concern that some people, adults as well as children, may already be becoming over-dependent on the computers they use, even to the extent of regarding them almost as substitutes for friends.

In this sense it is always worth asking not only whether computers may restrict the richness of our language, but also whether in answering that objection software developers might contribute to far more disturbing consequences – many more people may come to regard computers as 'friends', and their relationships with their fellow human beings may be even more threatened. Is it better to accept that computers require us to use special kinds of convention in language (which makes them suitable for particular kinds of logical applications) than to make the language which they can use so close to our own that we can easily slip into the trap of regarding them as intelligent, even sensitive, beings? Given the relentless research to make computers simulate human behaviour it may be that in society at large we will not be offered an explicit choice. It is not difficult to imagine that at some stage many people may feel the need to reject completely all modern technology if such developments were to lead, as Papert has suggested, to widespread psychosis in children, and indeed in adults too.[14]

If, however, we always ensure that we are actively aware of the weaknesses as well as the strengths of computers as tools, then it is difficult to see how our use of them could do anything but enrich the range of modes of both language and thinking which are open to us.

Hijacking the computer as a subversive device

Anyone who values creativity cannot fail to be disturbed by the fact that computers are appearing in schools at a time when there is a growing convergence of outlook among educators and the public that the main goal of education is to develop the concrete operational skills of technical reason coupled with functional, utilitarian 'skills' in language. The current reification of technique reflects a belief that the only important learning is that which can be precisely described in quantifiable terms ('the Basics'): it is a value system which champions instrumental reason at the expense of human values. And the computer is a powerful tool for technocrats who think like this; it takes no imagination and little effort to make the computer function as a monitor of mechanical operations.

But this is no justification for rejecting the tool: rather, it demands the raising of our consciousness of the biases of all technologies, and a positive discrimination in favour of using them, where appropriate, to meet genuine needs. It may be that computers were launched in schools as an 'educational technology' for narrow curricular goals, but they are ripe for hijacking as subversive devices by enlightened educators concerned with increasing the autonomy of children as learners. The use of the computer as a writing tool is an outstanding example of such a liberating application. Rather than simply washing our hands of computers because we do not like much of what we see (which is still a widespread reaction amongst teachers in Britain), we will be far more effective if instead we demonstrate that it is at least possible to use computers in ways which can extend the potential of all of us as learners. The critical factor is our attitude towards both technology and the nature of learning. In schools as they are today, it is amongst primary school teachers and teachers of English in the secondary schools that some hope may lie for the appropriate use of the computer as a liberating tool rather than a child-processor or a 'purpose' for which children must be prepared.

In an atmosphere full of extravagant claims about the latest technologies one message above all deserves to be remembered: whatever its applications the computer should be treated as just another tool like the pen or the typewriter, just another medium like books or television. If only, in our attachment to 'creativity', we were to be more conscious that tools can have as great a place in the service of the imagination as in the performance of technical operations: sculptors, as well as plumbers, use tools.

This book provides a variety of perspectives which may provide some points of departure for those who are new to the field, but we need to explore for ourselves the special characteristics of the computer as a tool and medium – not simply from the perspective of teachers of English and language arts, but more broadly from the standpoint of people deeply committed to the value of reading, writing, talking and listening. Whatever standpoint teachers in schools choose to adopt, there can be little doubt that the spread of computer-based technologies in the world at large will have profound effects on the attitude of children towards the nature and function of the written word.

2 Young Writers and the Computer

MICHAEL CLARK

It is no longer considered heretical – or even unorthodox – to suggest that schools undervalue writing. And yet it still seems rather a strange view to put forward. Given the vast amount of time, energy (and paper) devoted to developing and exercising this arcane skill, can it really be that schools have got it wrong, again? It seems likely that we have.

At primary level children lurch across great expanses of unlined paper, taking as long as two years (or even more) to achieve adequate neuro-muscular control over their recalcitrant pencils. In the meantime they are obliged to filter the richness and wonder of their imaginative response to the world through crabbed and convoluted script. Of course primary teachers are aware of the importance of talk, and of course the availability of the tape-recorder, the big paintbrush, and so on, do permit other kinds of record to be made. But the centrality of the written word in the educational system cannot be denied. The failure of some children to make what is considered adequate progress is a particular feature of the primary classroom which causes both children and teachers alike great concern. And even at best, with children who do learn to write fairly well, this 'writing' may well chain the imagination rather than release it in those early years.

Nor would anyone maintain that things are any better at secondary level. Despite the admirable advances in curriculum development, in examination syllabus requirements and, more fundamentally, in teachers' attitudes to language, both spoken and written, problems remain. Writing still generates its own '3 Rs': Repeat (as in 'copy from the board . . .'); Re-gurgitate (as in 'Write me an essay on . . .'); and Reject (as in 'rule off, turn over the page and put this new heading . . .'). Writing is all too often a control mechanism — the copying of notes or, worse still, worksheets, does keep the class quiet. And it fills up the books — neatly. Writing is fre-quently an inefficient way of transferring information from one place (the teacher's book) to another place (the child's book) via a third place (the blackboard). The information itself makes about as much difference to either teacher or child as it does to the blackboard. Worse still, writing in school is often a gigantic confidence trick, a conspiracy of teacher and child condoned by the examination system and rarely challenged. Tasks are set which encourage the young writer to mimic a display of apparent power over information. Answering the individual examination question, producing the appropriate six or seven hundred word essay, implies that this competence in presenting (more or less) the required information indicates a more general ability to store, select and manipulate information — of various kinds — as appropriate. The implication is that children understand. All too often this is a deceit, and teachers share in this deception.

A goal for the educative process might be to ensure that 'data becomes information becomes knowledge becomes wisdom by the exercise of intelligence and sensitivity through experience'. It is a goal rarely reached in schools. Moreover, the paltry attempts schools make to trap, to record, to present and then to assess any of these stages in the 'getting of wisdom' by writing things down serves to compound the difficulties facing the individual child. There are the mechanics of writing, the conventions, the need for corrections and therefore rewriting. All that is daunting enough. Then there is another problem: you write before and while you think, and the writing changes what you think, only now you've already written it . . . . The wonder is that anyone ever writes anything worth reading.

And so, finally, we come to the fact that it is what we read that determines what we think about our own writing. Obviously enough, and centrally, this applies to content, but there is something else. We read, and children read, the printed word. Handwriting is ephemeral, domestic or perhaps intimate. It is rarely public or authoritative. The printed word is one more insidious, all-pervasive aspect of our hidden curriculum. The status of content is largely determined by the form of presentation. And so teachers have an obsession with straight lines, margins, neatness, consistent, acccurate spelling and punctuation. Behind all these is the unacknowledged model – the printed, not the hand-written word. But hand-writing – even when well produced – is still only a poor imitation of print. This is why children, particularly those who have difficulties with writing, will spend an inordinate amount of time making a fair copy of indifferent work – and react violently to the least error, preferring to rip out a page and start again rather than accepting that the smallest mistake should remain.

Teachers seem to find it worthwhile to allocate a considerable amount of their own time (even when little better than two-fingered typists themselves) to ensure that children do see their writing 'in print', even if that print is only spirit-duplicated typescript. For print gives to the writing not only that clarity of presentation which is the characteristic of the book or newspaper: it also lends an air of authority – possibly spurious – to what is written. But for most children, most of the time, their writing is not so presented. Once complete, all that remains is usually the memory of mistakes made and corrected – and a mark. The content pales into insignificance compared with those two features, the error and the mark. These two rapidly combine within the school system to create an impact as great as the influence of print itself. The mistake has moral overtones of sin and guilt. Avoiding the mistake becomes even more important than the quality of what is notionally correct. And since the teacher is the person who identifies the error and awards the mark, then the game can rapidly become pleasing teacher rather than creating anything worthwhile.

Inaccessible models, spurious learning, error-obsessed children (and teachers): it all seems rather depressing. And they are all long-standing preoccupations with the English-teaching profession. But even where teachers are able to challenge and transform such a bleak non-educational environment and process, it remains true that they have to expend a very considerable amount of time, energy and ingenuity to do so: time and energy which could well be directed more productively.

Few English teachers would have suspected that the 'micro' would be able to provide any kind of help or support in their perennial search for more effective teaching strategies. And yet, surprisingly enough, it appears that the arrival of a micro in an English classroom can be a powerful agent of change.

A micro in the classroom: what do you need?

Experience shows that a computer alone is not enough. For the English teacher a printer is essential. In addition, although it is possible to work from cassette, a disc-drive makes loading and saving both programs and text much faster and less prone to error. Certainly at secondary level the constraints of the average school timetable mean that without a disc-drive effective classroom use of a computer for English teaching is virtually impossible.

The required system – computer, VDU, disc-drive and printer is sometimes known as a 'work station'. It is generally agreed that unless a class has regular access to at least one work-station, preferably in the same classroom, there is little chance that the computer will have any real impact on children.

The first task, then, is to gain access to a work-station. That in itself may be a major undertaking, especially at secondary level, leading to a significant shift in the school power structure. Most BBC B machines at secondary level, for example, according to Acorn (the manufacturers of the BBC computer) are located within Science departments – though one would suspect probably not purchased from departmental funds.

Suggesting that a computer is actually a data-handling device rather than merely a number cruncher may cause some ripples within a school. Unease is likely to grow if the argument continues that, since most data in schools is text-based, it makes sense to look at micros primarily as text-handling machines and therefore it is logical to locate them with those departments who consider text as of particular importance. British teachers in secondary schools may find it useful to bear in mind that Business Studies Departments may already have made significant progress in this area and that effective and fruitful interdepartmental co-operation may be possible, particularly if there has been a significant injection of funding (as with TVEI in Britain). Assuming that particular battle can be fought and won, and that the all-important printer is also available for some of the time, the English teacher is likely to find that the first essential additional purchase is a word-processing package.

Word-processing packages

A word-processing (WP) package – the program and associated documentation – may be on tape or disc but at best will be on a chip which can be permanently installed into the computer and is then available immediately with no time-lag for loading or possibility of damage to cassette or floppy disc. In Britain prices range from around £5 (for something like TASWORD 2 for the Spectrum) up to £150 for the near professional standard of SUPERSCRIPT (Commodore). Programs for the BBC B (EDWORD, WORDWISE, VIEW) currently retail between £40 and £60.

A WP package gives four essential facilities. First, it transforms the computer keyboard into an electric typewriter with the VDU as a display. What you type is (usually) what you see. Second, it enables you to correct – by deletion or insertion – what you have typed without having to rub out, blank out, throw away or do any of the other tedious and infuriating things that happen when typing on an ordinary typewriter. Thirdly it usually enables you to establish – and alter – the layout and organization of text (including moving blocks of text around in most programs) by means of fairly simple commands. Finally, and most importantly, it enables you to print out (or store) the finished version of your typed work.

Personal choice will determine to some extent which WP package you select but, for British teachers, it seems to be felt that in the £40–60 range EDWORD offers the clearest teaching manual and most on-screen help regarding commands. VIEW has the most sophisticated range of commands; WORDWISE is the most straightforward to use.

The key features to consider are:

1 Does the writing you see on screen print out in exactly the same way on paper? Some programs have a 40-column display (i.e. effectively

40 characters in a line) but print 80 columns (or more). It is usually possible to use a command which will provide you with an on-screen display showing how the writing will look when printed out, but it can be confusing if you have to switch from one display to another.

2 How much text will the computer store before the memory is full? If all you want is one-page essays or worksheets, a small memory store won't matter. If you want to encourage work on much longer texts that need to be instantly available to allow for scanning, selecting and reorganization, then memory size may become crucial.

3 Is the information displayed on screen clear, unambiguous and helpful?

4 Similarly, how good (i.e. clear, accurate and succinct) is the documentation? In this area, as in so much of computing, documentation isn't always suited to the naïve user.

Printers

The point has already been made that you need to be able to save children's writing and print it out. Most programs have options for saving to disc or tape and for printing to either serial or parallel printers. You may have to learn a little about how computers work in order to cope with setting up a printer but there is usually at least one friendly computer person in the school, operating in the role of sharer rather than scarer, to whom you can turn.

You also need a printer. Again, while it is possible to cope with a little Spectrum or Cumana printer (for between £50 and £70 in Britain), they offer only 40-column printout and you really need a printer which will give at least 80 columns – so that your printed text fits neatly onto standard typing paper.

A dot-matrix printer will cost between £100 and perhaps £350 and will be fast, relatively quiet and give clear print. Dot-matrix printers may also offer facilities for printing out in different typefaces (even different languages), graphics (both illustrations and mapwork) and a variety of other options. Daisy-wheel printers are slower, more noisy (on the whole) and more expensive (up to £600). However, they offer a range of typefaces (one daisy-wheel to buy for each) which are very clear and even closer to 'book' print than dot-matrix. But any printer is better than none.

In the classroom

Unless you have regular access to a work-station (i.e., for part of the week or a regular number of lessons) or, still better, one permanently available in the classroom, then the teacher will end up using WP facilities rather like an enhanced typewriter. It will still be a case of working on the machine in your 'spare' time to process children's writing. More importantly the young writer is still being denied access to, and therefore control over, the essential means of production.

The only real solution is a permanent work-station. The printer can be shared but the rest of the facility needs to be readily available. Computing across the curriculum is just that: computers spread throughout the school not locked away in one or more rooms or welded to rows of desks for something called 'computer appreciation' classes.

The computer and the class

There are still some logistical difficulties, however. One computer and one keyboard implies only one child working at a time. It is possible to have groups of children working with a single keyboard but this requires a high level of organization and classroom management and considerable self-discipline on the part of children. Like mixed-ability teaching, this new approach initially creates as many problems as it solves.

In addition, the children still have to learn to use the keyboard. There is a great danger that we are about to produce a generation of two-fingered typists who can hammer away on a QWERTY keyboard, correcting mistakes as they go along, producing printed-out work considerably better, in appearance, than the average exercise book – but still working in a most inefficient manner. Effective use of the keyboard needs to be taught as yet another classroom skill and the fact that people can 'get by' without becoming really competent is really sidestepping the issue.

At primary level, however, it is not at all clear that very young children have the finger span to cope with the QWERTY keyboard. Comparisons with music teaching would obviously be fruitful here. Moreover, it is a moot point whether the conventional ways of teaching the QWERTY keyboard (generally mechanical drills and tests which are to typing what 'a, ab, ac, ad, af' are to the teaching of reading) really have much place in the lively, person-oriented classroom of the good primary school. This could mean that both the younger child and the over-eager enthusiasts of all ages could be denied access to micro facilities because of inappropriate or insufficient keyboards. Fortunately there is an alternative, a new keyboard with a revolutionary new approach which offers simultaneous access for up to five children working on a BBC computer (and probably on Spectrum and Commodore 64 by the time this book is published).

Quinkey

Quinkey is a new British keyboard designed to interface with the BBC computer and derived from the hand-held business word-processing device known as a Microwriter.[1] The keyboard employs only five major keys plus a command key. Yet it can generate the full alphabet, punctuation, numerics and so on, duplicating virtually all of the BBC keyboard if required to do so.

Quinkey keyboards can be bought separately but are particularly intended for classroom use in sets of four which can be linked directly to a BBC computer. With associated software it is possible for four children to work on their own individual WP tasks simultaneously with independent storage, display and printout facilities for each child. Both screen display, storage and keyboard combinations can be varied and the QWERTY keyboard can also be incorporated within the system. With different software it is theoretically possible to access most programs requiring 31K or less of memory space from any one of the connected keyboards.

Children as young as six can span the Quinkey's keyboard with little difficulty and preliminary studies suggest that children can reach handwriting speed with Quinkey in about a third of the time it takes with QWERTY. The combinations of keys required to produce letters are related to letter shapes and again preliminary investigation suggests that the more limited neuro-muscular control necessary to form letters is midway between the single keypress of the QWERTY and the more complex motor control of a pencil. Moreover, learning is easier because of the relationship between the pattern of keys and the letter shape.

A major study involving some eleven schools, both primary and secondary, forty teachers and over a thousand children began in Newcastle-upon-Tyne in September 1984 as a follow-up to pioneering work done in the city over the last two years. Some twenty thousand pounds will be spent to provide the permanent work stations required in both primary and secondary schools. It will thus be possible to consider the impact of word-processing on classes when the facility is readily available and look in addition at the particular features of Quinkey in terms of rates of learning, retention and its special place for children with learning difficulties.

The particular advantage of Quinkey, other than its unique keyboard, is without doubt the fact that the software QUAD marketed with the keyboard, splits the screen into up to five windows and splits available memory in the same way so that a group of children can work on their text individually or co-operatively, finally saving and/or printing out their work independently. With Quinkey one computer can be used by an entire group and thus fits neatly into the conventional patterns of small group activities (still sadly more prevalent at primary than secondary level in Britain). It is the availability of a technology which complements normal school practice rather than requiring a major readjustment which is so attractive and, until add-on QWERTY keyboards with associated software become available, it is hard to think of any other more cost-effective alternative to aid the use of WP in the classroom.

The more controversial claims made by Quinkey proponents in relation to ease of learning and typing speed need further investigation.

The impact of WP

It is a very special experience to introduce WP to a class, particularly if there are children for whom writing has, until then, been a disappointing chore resulting in failure rather than success.

Text suddenly moves from exercise book to TV screen – that alone enhances its appearance. It also highlights errors. But those very errors which caused so much trouble before are suddenly amenable to correction. Instead of requiring embarrassing crossing out or tedious rewriting a single keypress remedies the situation. The ease and speed with which writing is printed out – the pleasure and, indeed initial disbelief with which the writing is greeted – emphasize the importance of giving children access to the means of production. They are no longer passive consumers of the written word. Teachers and children alike become producers: they make books.

Paradoxically perhaps, access to such instant perfection in print makes children more rather than less critical. There seem to be a number of reasons for this. A printed version distances the writer from the act of creation – however modest that act might be. With distancing comes the ability to exercise an editorial function more dispassionately. Critical observations become precise and exact. It is, of course, far easier to see a mistake (and more difficult to conceal one). But since it is so easy to correct errors, pupils become more ready to admit that the mistakes exist. The reward for correcting something is no longer an invitation to copy it out again. Effort is directed only to the error. The machine takes care of the rest. Suddenly punctuation becomes of real interest. It is a delight to listen to 7-year-olds arguing over the alternative positions for speech marks or an impassioned defence of the placing of a comma – and it does happen.

Surprisingly, too, at primary level children seem to return to their 'ordinary' (hand) writing with renewed interest, and it does improve. Nor is there any reduction in the amount children are prepared to write by hand. On the contrary, they seem willing to write more because it is seen as being valued more highly.

Some concern has been expressed that children tend to restrict their correction of errors to the individual letter or word, rather than looking at the structure of their writing and the opportunity that WP provides for more substantial alteration and manipulation of text. But this limitation is not really surprising. Until the arrival of the micro it has hardly been feasible to encourage large numbers of children to undertake the writing of really substantial texts. Consequently a consideration of the structure of the novel (or even extended short story) has been essentially passive, as reader rather than writer. In the same way, the only model a young writer might seek to emulate has been the teacher. Teacher corrections, for good reason, have tended to be at the level of letter or word. A global comment or suggestion at the end of a piece of work might have more general implications but this is still, sadly, the exception rather than the rule. With such a model can we wonder that children are rather timid in their response to the potential of the technology?

Word-processing and the future

The need now is for extended studies to examine precisely what happens when a WP facility is available. Will young writers always merely tinker with punctuation and spelling? Is it the case that the only use of the micro is to produce 'fair copy' of writing already composed in exercise book or on file paper? If this is so then the micro may make life a little easier for the over-worked teacher, but could one really argue that the expenditure was justified? It is still possible to buy a considerable number of books for the money required to purchase one work-station. The question must be: are there ways in which teachers might modify both their teaching style and the tasks they set in their quest to make children more effective writers, to ensure that the learning situation established takes full advantage of the micro?

There is always the danger that the preferences and prejudices of the teachers in this, as in so many other situations, may produce yet another hidden curriculum with its own new orthodoxy. Already you can hear observations like 'WP is all very well for factual writing, but for anything "really creative", particularly poetry, I just couldn't use a machine'. How far is our love affair with the pencil merely convention? What happens when words 'dance in light' and you can 'swim through text' to quote two alternative metaphors for the liberating effect of WP.

Extended writing, with initial chapters revised and redrafted as later chapters make more demands on the structure and content of text, is one area ripe for exploration. The literary essay obviously lends itself to WP work. At last the missing quotation or misplaced paragraph can be dealt with, but not at the cost of having to retype an entire essay. It even becomes realistic to consider, on a regular basis, alternative ways of ordering the same set of paragraphs produced as a tentative response to some essay title. Note-taking can now be translated to the screen and notes can be altered and reconstituted in a way never before possible.

Using Quinkey sets in conjunction with a conventional WP package, one child can print text on the screen and other users – children or teachers – can intervene to alter the text. Somehow the cursor manipulation is far less threatening than marginal comments or red ink. Not least perhaps because if the suggested alteration is no better you can always reinsert the original version.

The vexing question of whether notes 'make sense' is easier to demonstrate as well. A printout of notes, separated from the screen and the original context, is readily available. In short, things we did before can now be done more easily, more rapidly and with less stress on child or teacher. That is all to the good. And some may say that is quite sufficient. After all, there is still room for improvement in writing in schools with our current understanding of the process and what is involved.

But micros can do more. New developments in software lead us into areas which we are only beginning to be able to define and describe.

The convention is now to divide the series of events which begin with the germ of an idea and end with a written text being addressed to a particular audience into three stages – pre-writing, writing and revision (or editing). The labels differ, the meanings given to the labels differ, and the divisions are to some extent arbitrary and of limited use. They serve, however, to focus attention on three aspects of this continuum of creativity, and it is possible to relate developments within computing to writing viewed in this way.

Inevitably the more sophisticated and powerful programs are only available for larger machines – in some cases only for very large machines indeed, well beyond the range of the budgets of the largest schools. However, experience tells us that costs of both hardware and software will fall, and with the increase in the number of links between different sorts of computers through various kinds of networking, it may be that schools will have access to far more powerful machines and associated software sooner than we think.

Prewriting

Just as a WP package may be of particular use to a child who cannot yet cope with the mechanics of handwriting, there are a number of programs which help cope with the basic structural organization of sentences.

The student is asked to provide lexical items in appropriate categories (noun, modifier and so on), although usually by example rather than by label. The program will then generate sentences using appropriate patterns and items. This kind of text may be, in effect, a 'story' or it may be presented as a poem. In addition the program may give the student the opportunity of performing transformations on structures: turning statements to questions, active to passive, singular to plural, and so on.

The most easily available program of this kind in the UK will be

GRAM by Mike Sharples for the BBC computer (although it is not yet published commercially). In the US, COMPUPOEM by Stephen Marcus uses the same techniques to generate text which echo haiku in their form and content.[2]

Writing

We have already considered the mainstream WP packages available in the UK and similarly available in the US although precise organization, format and facilities in American systems like BANK STREET WRITER may differ slightly. The WP package is essentially a writing aid, enabling the user to create on screen, usually with more ease, what would normally be developed with pencil or pen.

Rewriting/editing

The next range of software seeks to aid the prospective author who has a text, but is dissatisfied with it.

There is insufficient evidence to determine whether or not the existence of a 'spelling checker' program helps or hinders the development of that particular aspect of writing ability. By analogy with calculators in relation to the teaching of mathematics it can be argued that a spelling checker shifts the focus of attention to more important aspects of writing.

It is also found that WP packages in general seem to make pupils more interested in spelling, and if a checker signals the existence of an error before actually providing the correct spelling this gives the writer a chance to make the necessary correction before calling on the machine to provide the answer. This is a 'safe' kind of speculation and the fact that there is instant reinforcement (or correction) ought to encourage good spelling habits.

It is also possible to develop spelling programs which give progressively more precise prompts as to the correct version of a misspelt word. For example, when the computer comes across a misspelling, e.g. 'peice', it might display these responses to the student:

- This spelling isn't in my dictionary.
- Do you mean a small bit of something?
- Do you know of any rules about the letters 'i', 'e' and 'c'?
- Can you see the difference between 'piece' and 'peice'?

Sophisticated programs provide large predefined dictionaries, allow for substantial specialist additions and will provide automatic correction. However, the more elaborate options cost commercial prices – up to £150 for something like SUPERSPELL or the resources of a University mainframe supporting the editorial options within UNIX. More modest software like WORDSPELL and SPELLCHECK, compatible with text generated by WP packages such as WORDWISE and VIEW retails at around £15. There remains a lot of work to be done, however, regarding the impact of such programs on writing.

Vocabulary and Stylistic Checks

Thesaurus options are available on some mainframe machines under UNIX and this will provide alternatives to words selected by the author both during the actual composition of a text or at the end in association with a word count and word check which signals repeated use of any particular item.

Elementary grammatical checkers and what pass for stylistic checks are also available, although generally requiring machines at the mini and mainframe level, not micros. Thus it is possible for machines to signal such 'ungrammatical' occurrences as singular subject with plural verb or to be programmed to recognize infelicitous phrases – excessive use of the passive, ending sentences with prepositions, and other neatly definable variants. Such software emanates in the main from the American tradition which considers language and the teaching of 'style' in a way which might be defined as mechanistic compared with British traditions.

Programs such as EPISTLE (IBM), WRITER'S WORKBENCH (Bell) and developments by Westinghouse and the US Navy all indicate how these ideas may be developed, but are currently beyond the range of school expenditure or use.

Beyond the editor: the intelligent word-processor

There are significant long-term implications of identifying units for correction or alteration which are larger than the single word. The end result of such a software development will be, it is anticipated, the intelligent word-processor.

As well as offering current facilities for presenting, correcting and moving text it will offer a system of analysis, comparison, substitution and manipulation of units of text far more sophisticated and flexible than is currently available. A 'unit of text' might be a phrase, sentence, paragraph or page. It may be defined according to syntactic or semantic criteria operating from the level of individual grammatical features up to supra-sentential units. Options and alternatives could be defined from within the computer's own banks of alternatives or the individual may be able to try out alternatives which result in the substitution of units throughout an extended text with appropriate structural alternatives.

Author systems

There is a further area of software development which doesn't really fit into any of these categories. These developments are not (simply) resources for the manipulation of syntactic or semantic units. They don't merely reflect back what the user writes. They don't signal errors (however defined) or provide alternatives at the level of word or structure. They are something different.

The American term 'author systems' may seem a little grandiose at present to British readers but the potential of this kind of program is very considerable. The principle is simple. A story may be considered as a sequence in which there occur a series of choices. At each point in the story the choice made will, to a certain extent, determine what might happen next. In story generators this approach enables pupils to create narrative of increasing complexity.

In a fairly simple example like STORY TREE there are six routes 'through' a story. At each branching point the choice made determines the story format. But this is only the simplest form. Much more elaborate software already exists for creating story settings, narrative choices and even characters of considerable complexity.

The model here is the adventure game, well known to computer enthusiasts, in which the user directs the computer through a complex world, often full of magic and fantasy, to collect certain objects, perform certain tasks and reach a particular goal. It is now possible to buy software which will create such programs for the user to play. These range from MY ADVENTURE to THE QUILL and Chelsea College's STORYMAKER (a version of Chandler's ADVENTURER design). Nor is it any longer the case that these must be bound by the 'dungeons and dragons' format. The development of other software based on everything from Sherlock Holmes through political satire to ecological disaster, some with elaborate sound and graphics, even an accompanying sound track and script, show how the authoring programs will develop.

These programs currently require a variable degree of skill in understanding the organization and structure of programming. Moreover, they tend to suffer from documentation which assumes a fairly high level of understanding. However, such problems of interpretation and communication are not insoluble.

What is important from the point of view of developing ability in writing is this option which allows the writer to follow through a range of alternative possibilities to complete a story. This could have significant consequences for the development of narrative. No longer will we assume that there is one ending and that only a Hardy or a John Fowles may provide alternatives. The notion of a quite different kind of collaboration between reader and author becomes possible if it is the reader's choices which determine the ultimate shape and sequence of one version of a story. It remains to be seen whether giving authors the power to provide a range of alternative ways of presenting and exploring their material will be of benefit.

But what about the mistake?

There remains the need to ensure that mistakes, false starts, even the genuine 'essays', are not lost simply because they are overwritten. We may want to be able to store and recall errors and initial tries to varying degrees of complexity and depth of recall – and how pleasant if all those alternatives come out well-typed instead of in the illegible scribble that almost always characterizes that last phrase squeezed in on the edge of the paper.

Stephen Marcus has done some work with 'invisible writing', in which the computer users adjusted screen brightness so that they could not see what they were writing as they first tried to put their thoughts into words. This reversal of the normal writer's block actually seemed helpful – largely because students weren't bothered by mistakes (the mistake again!) which they normally felt obliged to go back and correct to the detriment of their getting down the flow of their initial ideas. Nor, at a more sophisticated level, were they as inhibited by premature worries about whether what they were writing 'made sense'. Invisible writing helped to remove some of the limitations which conventional writing techniques impose on the creative process.[3] There are certain to be other ways forward.

Conclusion

The micro is not a threat to writing. It is a liberating influence, a powerful tool and, perhaps, a starting point for new ways of using language. Like computer applications in other areas of society, the new technology and supporting software can be used to support existing power structures, to maintain current bad practice, and to limit experiment and development. As always the challenge to that danger and the source of a solution is a human solution: ourselves.

3 Electronic Text: a Choice Medium for Reading?

BRENT ROBINSON

and

EDWARD B. VERSLUIS

In Book I of Homer's *Odyssey*, Penelope tearfully chides the minstrel Phemios for singing the bitter tale of the homecoming of the Greeks from Troy. This scene is the first direct appearance of Penelope in the work, clearly exhibiting her abiding grief over the absence of her husband. It is also one of the earliest depictions in literature of a choice exercised by audiences since time immemorial: not to have a distressing tale continue.

Until now, deciding whether or not to let the tale continue was about all the audiences of oral and written literature could do to express their curiosity in–and satisfaction with–the progress of an account. With the advent of computerized text storage and display, however, the relationship of the audience to the tale, of the reader to the text, is beginning to change in complex and far-reaching ways. The power not merely to stop but actually to alter the course of the story as it unfolds is only one of a number of options made available by the new electronic medium. The consequences of such freedom include both problems and possibilities for all concerned with maintaining, enriching or simply participating in a literate culture. For teachers and learners, it is a situation full of import and ambiguous opportunity.

The implications of computerized text display can be roughly divided into two areas: the influence on traditional literature and the influence on traditional literacy. Some of those implications are unavoidable; others are merely potential in the medium. As teachers we ought to exercise our ability to ease the constraints and exploit the potential of this electronic text medium. It would be foolhardy to deny or neglect this. We cannot smash the new electronic 'presses'; the pressures which have brought us to the start of a new print era are too great. But there is no need for us to adopt a defensive stance for there ought to be no threat. Of course, there will be ramifications in our culture as electronic text becomes more widely used. It is a new medium with its own characteristics which will have important consequences for literate users – it may affect their facility in the reading process; it may alter their concepts of the nature of print material in general and of literature in particular; it may have other, possibly less obtrusive, effects upon the social, political and economic structure of a society which is dependent upon the free and efficient passage of information. But we have experienced such radical innovations before and we should consider the most recent typographic development constructively. We can see the dramatic alterations to our whole social and cultural fabric which followed Gutenberg. We can look back on the less drastic but still significant effects caused by the launch of the first paperback books. Those technological advances contributed to the spread of literacy rather than militated against it. Arguably, for many readers, they also enhanced the nature of the medium they propagated.

Implications for the printed word

Even if for ecological, economic or some other reason, electronic text were to supersede paper copy (which is by no means certain and is certainly not advocated here), it must be remembered that the electronic medium would still be dependent upon the printed word. The culture it serviced would still be a literate culture. Moreover, it would be a culture based on a textual medium which, technologically, could offer considerable compensations for the loss of paper copy. So, in our present society, the emergence of electronic text alongside conventional books and other 'hard copy', rather than in place of them, ought only to enrich what the print medium already has to offer. This chapter attempts to outline the nature of that enrichment and some of the ways in which teachers, together with sympathetic software designers, should prepare students to accept and exploit the new text medium.

To do this, we need to amend and extend present definitions and preconceptions about the print medium. To give a few brief and fundamental examples: information is no longer printed permanently in black on white; no longer can we assume that what we have read is immutable, for we need constantly to skim over each frame of text to see if it has been updated anywhere; we cannot even 'Begin at the beginning ... and go on till you come to the end: then stop'. Even the linear sequence of words, argument or narrative need no longer necessarily apply to electronic text.

Literature is sometimes envisaged as beginning and ending at the margins of the printed or written page. The inadequacy of confining literature to one medium was pointed out long ago by people who were aware of oral poetry and filmed drama. Nevertheless, the mainstay of even oral and filmed productions today is the written text. And it is here where we can begin to examine more closely several features which can be altered when that same text is mediated by a computer.

In the first place, traditional print tends to appear before the reader in dark static blocks upon the constant page. Those blocks are rendered even more dark and static in direct proportion to their magnitude and density. Open a book at any page and the print is there – as it always has been. On the other hand, computerized text is dynamic from the moment it appears. Switch on a visual display unit and text emerges from a blank void as the cathode ray tube becomes active. Press a key or run a program – almost any program in any subject area – and further text appears to fill the screen. And even when the luminous text appears, it is limited by the narrow confines of the glass surface and must be read with an awareness that it may instantly alter or disappear. In its place, instead of the sober regimentation of bound pages, there stands the potential of not one, but an array of radically divergent displays, each summoned in direct response to previous actions by the user.

Computers are very fast manipulators of text. We can contemplate a microcomputer with memory sufficient to hold a whole book, complete with a number of parallel, alternative narratives. Already, a mainframe computer or even a microcomputer coupled to a videodisc machine can be programmed to retrieve any single page or 'frame' of text in any number of sequences from thousands of such frames in a matter of seconds. The reader's experience remains essentially as linear as it was with the traditional text, and still involves thinking which is both retrospective (comparing recently acquired information with what has gone before) and anticipatory (calculating the nature and probability of what is yet to come). But in place of a single, well-defined progression within the computer program, there is now the possibility of many paths, each one beckoning insistently as it flashes upon the screen.

If the computerized text displayed is bright, transitory and subject to rapid changes of context, there is an inducement for the writer to reduce further the amount of text displayed at any given moment. Shorter selections allow a certain exploitation of both the transitory and multidirectional aspects of text flow.

One other effect of shortening selections of text is to release increasing amounts of space for graphics. At the moment, graphics can take up disproportionally large amounts of computer memory. This will be solved in the long term as internal and external memory storage capacity increases. Meanwhile, given that more storage space could be made available for illustrations and diagrams, their inclusion in programmed textual material could be increased dramatically. In conventional books, graphic material tends to be kept to a minimum because it adds significantly to publication costs. There is no such economic differential between text and image in electronic displays.

Why graphics? Medieval monks probably illuminated their painstakingly copied manuscripts in the same fashion they would have decorated any object as precious and significant as a book. Whatever their motives, the result of their labours was a charming enhancement to the text. Computer graphics can achieve that effect too. At the same time, the inclusion of graphics could go some way towards minimizing a medieval legacy which some readers do feel – an awesome reverence for experience embodied in permanent print. This response can result in intimidation or alienation from the print medium itself. The ephemerality and potential dynamism of electronic print could contribute to a lessening of this hostile reaction which many readers, particularly the less fluent, now bring to text. The characteristics of the new medium many readers – among them, the barely literate – will have seen before. As an amusement machine, a larger number of readers will have already mastered many of the medium's intricacies in arcade, bar or coffee shop. Electronic print, ephemeral and dynamic, could be used by teachers as a substitute for books to encourage a more positive disposition towards print media where such a response has not been manifested before.

When we consider the quality of graphics in an arcade machine, we begin to appreciate how computers can present and animate illustrations in a way unavailable in conventional textual formats. Computers can furnish multicoloured illustrations much more cheaply than a book. Whereas a book must often present a series of static images to convey a process, a computer can animate a single display and show the same information more succinctly. Computers can offer graphics either alone or with text, concurrently or sequentially, static or animated. It is obvious that the option is open in computer software for graphics to be powerful, even indispensible aids to meaning.

Implications for literature

Besides alterations in the text display itself, the computer opens up another area of perhaps even greater potential. This is the transaction between the audience and the text, or more precisely, between the reader and the writer. Once, in the traditional print medium, the writer made many decisions which, when strung out on the printed page, the reader either chose to follow or, like Penelope, to avoid entirely. Now the author has the power to challenge the reader at every point to make all sorts of significant choices without disrupting the flow of the text.

For fictional texts, this means that writers are now permitted to enter into a sort of collaboration with their readers. The writer is still responsible for making the initial decisions about where and in what fashion the text flow will begin. But thereafter, the writer's decisions could consist almost entirely of what choices to offer the reader, both in terms of different kinds and of different levels. Teachers have long urged their students to respond actively to texts placed before them. Typical reading and writing activities are often concerned with furthering comprehension, encouraging empathy with characters and aiding the subjective evaluation of experiences presented in the text. Such processes can be implicit in the negotiation of an electronic text. Such texts might be strewn with 'menu pages' from which to select the subsequent story line. Alternatively, readers might be allowed to express their preferences for the development of the narrative through periodic question and answer routines. In either case, the computer would respond on each occasion by branching to one of a series of alternative parallel texts. The situation has progressed far beyond Penelope's ability to call for another story. The audience can now be offered the option to modify, to any degree it sees fit, the various elements of what is essentially the same story.

Probably the most extreme version of the type of microworld which a reader can now build around himself through text is the very popular adventure program. This is no longer a story in the conventional sense at all, though it does embody a narrative potential. Here a situation is defined, the reader is identified as the protagonist and a quest is specified for his attainment. Thereafter, the readers/players are free to develop the narrative as they see fit. Typically, they specify an action (normally in the form of a verb plus a noun) which is met by a textual response from the computer. For example, if they decide to:

Take treasure

they may be confronted with:

There is a blinding flash and the door of the dungeon slams closed behind you.

What next?

At this stage they might type:

Open trap

As they continue to pursue their goals through this imaginary world, they shape the narrative.

This new power of the reader as dream-master has both positive and negative implications. The opportunity for vicarious experience has always drawn us to literature. Now that opportunity will be enlarged by the option of directing and refining the vicarious experience almost totally in the direction of wish fulfillment. Unattractive truths, disturbing visions, even glaring probability could soon be swept aside in a lunge for self-gratification. The expansion of opportunities for creativity, apparently a good thing in itself, could be turned to the ends of a base self-indulgence.

There is an obvious role for the teacher here in educating the tastes of young readers towards a more refined engagement with the text. There is also a ray of hope residing in the fact that computer use, unlike watching films or television, is not passive. Once satiety has been reached in those media, the experience still continues to roll on. The computer experience, in contrast, always calls for a choice on the part of the user. When the pleasure of dreams attained begins to fade, the user can be urged on to other things.

Implications for literacy

All this has touched on, and leads quite naturally into, the second major area of influence exerted by computerizing text – the influence on traditional literacy. Each of the text alterations possible with the use of a computer implies an effect upon the reader/user as well. In the past, print displays were essentially passive. They did not respond to the reactions of their readers. Incorporating microelectronic technology, not only the text itself, but also the text displays of the future, could be dynamic and interactive. They could respond and behave in relation to the reactions of their viewers (within, of course, the parameters with which they have been programmed). There is no reason why the readers' system of choices should not be extended to allow them (or teachers) to make constructive use of the dynamic factors offered by electronic print displays.

In the first place, the display medium is, at least potentially, an attractive one. For the most part at the moment, electronic text means the presentation of characters on a cathode-ray tube display, similar to that found on a commercial television receiver. This is light-generating and has very different properties from printed paper, which is light-reflecting. In the not too distant future, it is likely that technological advance will provide alternatives which may reduce some of the distraction of such generative displays. For example, liquid crystal displays (such as may be found on digital watches) are light-reflecting and thus have important presentational features in common with paper. Further development of these forms of display, to the point where they are capable of presenting larger quantities of text than at present, will return readers to a more familiar set of print characteristics. But until we have one or more viable alternatives to a cathode-ray tube, it is crucial that readers of electronic text are helped to use it effectively. Indeed, it could be argued that an awareness of such considerations ought to form part of our present concept of literacy and that a familiarity with them should constitute part of any school's reading curriculum. A large part of learning to be literate consists of learning how to perform the many tasks made possible by the unique characteristics of printed displays. This is particularly so for the acquisition of higher-order literacy skills. The new electronic medium, however, challenges even the beginning reader to acquire a much more sophisticated understanding and control of it.

At the outset, teachers should ensure that they appreciate the viewing conditions of screen reading in class. Research has shown that the viewing angle of a screen is critical. So, too, is distance between screen and reader. Problems of perception may be further exacerbated if the colour, contrast or brightness of the receiver or monitor are not well adjusted. Unlike conventional print, electronic print appears to be back-lit – that is, it emits direct light and does not depend on reflected light. It may thus be easily obscured by direct or bright ambient light. Good teachers will always bear these factors in mind whenever students are presented with electronic text. They will also ensure, over time, that the students themselves become consciously aware of these viewing factors and that they become well versed in constructing their own optimal viewing situations.

The legibility of electronic text is further hampered by the fact that, at the present time, some microcomputers display unfamiliar character fonts with suppressed ascenders and descenders, no proportional spacing of letters along the line, and short line lengths which can produce awkward breaks in words and sentences. They can offer also as few as 22 characters on which to let the eyes fixate. Most electronic print displays have only 24 or 25 lines to the frame. There is therefore a severe restriction on the space available for 'formatting' text. These limitations do not make reading easy for the early reader, prohibiting the provision of typographical and other clues. They make it equally difficult for the more advanced reader who may wish to skim-read the text. At all levels of reading, electronic text presents novel factors which affect the reading process. Yet these will not always present difficulties. A range of coloured foregrounds and backgrounds can already improve legibility. Some microcomputers already offer a variety of different fonts and line lengths. A few even allow programmers to design their own character sets. A very recent innovation has been the appearance of larger screens with proportionately greater textual capacity than the conventional video display. This has allowed greater spatial freedom for formatting texts for easy reading and for providing typographic signals.

In this context, it is interesting to note that spatial formatting of electronic print, unlike conventional print, does not expend amounts of storage space directly proportional to the space visible on display. Computers store print electronically in compact form with 'embedded commands' defining the layout of text. Extra indentations or inter-line spacing in a book soon increase its number of pages significantly. In an electronic memory, a twenty-line interval between units of text will take up no more than a brief coded command (perhaps some 10 characters or less) specifying the layout whenever the text is printed to screen or paper. With no arguments on grounds of economy of manufacture or of storage, it is quite possible for text designers and writers to adopt more ambitious designs for electronic print display. To give a brief example, the presentation of prose in short semantic units (not unlike verse in initial appearance but without left justification) could assist not only the less able reader but also the more able reader – especially where the latter might be wishing to apply a speed-reading strategy to a print medium which at the moment does not facilitate readability.

These options should not be open exclusively to software designers. Teachers could be given the opportunity at the outset of programs to select from proferred menus the particular type of textual display they require for users. There is also no reason why readers themselves should not be invited to determine their own displays. These readers are quite likely to be afforded a similar opportunity in the electronic books and other print communications of the future and they should now begin to appreciate and take responsibility for the display of their electronic reading matter. (For what is now a classic projection of one potential device of the future, the portable silicon chip reader, see *The Mighty Micro* by the late Chris Evans.) In time, perhaps even fluent readers could gain significantly from a provision for user-defined typographic variations like italic and boldface fonts, indentations and the use of colour and underlining, which they could use as directional signposts in annotating texts they wish to study.

One of the virtues of the printed page is the reader's ability to choose to linger over a particular detail. Given a personalized display like the one we have just envisaged, the possibility could be positively encouraged – even to the extent of highlighting the text or isolating it on the screen through enlargement, colour, spacing or one of a number of other facilities now available.

At the same time, however, it is also likely that electronic print displays will put a premium upon speedy and efficient comprehension. Sometimes, individual words and phrases appear anywhere on screen for only a brief period. Sometimes text is displayed letter-by-letter or line-by-line at a preset rate, successive lines of text frequently scrolling off the top of the screen. At other times whole frames of text are exposed and then replaced by others at short preset time intervals. Readers must learn to adopt the speed-reading strategies demanded by the situation. Even where the presentation of text is sufficiently lengthy, readers may still be encouraged to adopt speed-reading techniques. Where visual display screens act as 'on-line terminals' with information transmitted in 'real time', there may be arguments for shortening the period that the terminal is 'logged-on' to a 'host machine': the situation denies access to other users and may increase telephone and other transmission charges. Moreover, even if such conditions do not exist, faster reading is likely to be encouraged by the ephemeral and transitory nature of the medium and the small sections of text presented in any one display frame. The reader is urged to pursue an experience or an argument, not just in the next column, but awaiting, on a screen now totally hidden from view. The effect produced is much like that of some 'reading improvement' machines which present small units of moving text to press the reader on to attain greater and greater speeds of comprehension.

Full comprehension will thus imply new techniques. It is not just a matter of unavoidably quicker reading. Rather it is a case of specific reading strategies like skimming and scanning, of accurate initial perception and longer memory retention. Perhaps some of these skills will be fostered implicitly by the medium if students are given frequent access to it. It would be foolish to expect universal acquisition. Poor readers may need structured and explicit mediation by teachers. Even good readers may not be proficient in the new medium. Serious thought needs to be given to the software used. There may often be a case for software in all subjects to offer user control so that the rate of display can match the reader's ability. In some software, this might take the form of a delay device which waits for the user to press a key before proceeding. Sometimes, the rate of pause or delivery of text to screen could be determined at the beginning of the program. This would be particularly useful to teachers wishing to exhort students towards faster reading through a gradation of text presentation speeds in a structured reading programme.

All this emphasis on speed might seem to be discouraging readers from pausing to reflect upon the significance of the text while reading. First, it should be admitted that not every traditional text encourages reflection. Shallow novels, trite verse and dull functional texts encourage little mental performance of any sort. Inadequate computerized text is just as uninspiring. But there are also times, during the course of some software, when simply to select the next screenful of material requires deliberate reflection. The course of the entire program is, at those times, in the reader's hands. And one direction is probably much more desirable than another.

While a reader can suffer a lapse of attention, glazed eyes simply gliding down the pages of even a good book, the reader/user of computerized text is less likely to drift in thought as options implying directions of the reading experience flash upon the screen. These options might go much farther than simple decision points in a branching, 'tree-structured' text. While reading frames of text, an on-screen thesaurus or dictionary could be called upon at any point to clarify a text. Further interrogative features could be built into the programmed text allowing the reader to make further interactions with it. These facilities could be summoned by pressing special keys or by typing 'command words' during the reading/search process. To summon a dictionary definition, for example, the word 'Define' could be offered. 'Enlarge' might route a reader through a reinforcing loop of the same content material differently expressed or structured. Other forms of graphic presentation could also be available. Typing in the word 'Show' could summon a diagrammatic representation of the information embodied in the text. In such interactions, the burden of choice, implicit in an imaginative computerization of the reading experience, requires and rewards comprehension. Thus comprehension, the backbone of traditional literacy, could be expanded.

This applies not only to multi-faceted branching texts but to sequential texts as well. There are, of course, a large number of reading strategies. The proficient reader is one who can adopt a strategy suitable to the text before him and his requirements in reading it. For such a reader there are many occasions when he does not assimilate a text in linear fashion. Initially, it is quite likely that his attention will focus on only the first one or two paragraphs and on the conclusion in an attempt to establish topic, theme or style. Thereafter, the reader may decide to read the article in its entirety. Or he may skim the text looking for key words and topic sentences, only occasionally pausing to read discrete units of text in greater detail. If such text were presented in a computerized form, the reader would need to adopt a much more overt, active strategy. Because a computer screen can hold only a small number of words at any one time, this must have a profound effect on the nature of skim-reading and of scanning. A newspaper can be scanned and the relevant pieces identified very quickly. If a visual display unit can provide access to only about 1000 characters at any one time, the same process has to take much longer. It will also involve different eye movements and manual motor skills as the keyboard (or some other device) is activated to frame further portions of text on screen.

The way in which frames of text are replaced on screen in any software will thus be very important to readers. It will be particularly significant in an explicit approach to the teaching of reading. It could be argued that animating text in its delivery to screen rather than presenting static displays frame-by-frame will encourage certain higher-order reading strategies. So scrolling text could be seen to encourage readers to skim quickly through a text – though its role as an inducement towards retrospective glances at the text as well as anticipatory reading may be reasonably questioned. Moreover, even scrolling can retard access to the text for a fluent reader. Presenting a single continuous column of text is likely to encourage bidirectional eye movements rather than the multidirectional movements which occur with good readers as they peruse the several columns of a newspaper, magazine, poster or other large-format print displays. Perversely therefore, there may be a real danger that the electronic presentation of large units of text could actually militate against non-sequential reading strategies. Compared to, say, the body of text revealed on a single sheet of newspaper, the electronic medium imposes an artificial and narrow window on a very small unit of text. Whether this urges the reader to focus on every word or whether it urges him to skim over the material and to replace the text with the next frame (as was postulated above) we do not yet know.

It would be a different matter if the reader/user could make imaginative use of the medium's idiosyncracies. There could be positive advantages if appropriate software could be designed and implemented to encourage readers to scroll both vertically and horizontally over large textual displays (in the manner of some of the spreadsheet software currently available) or if it gave him access to a number of text windows so he could hold one on screen while calling up another in juxtaposition or if he could scroll two halves of a screen simultaneously or independently.

Implications for functional prose[1]

This paper has already outlined some of the ways in which the literary experience could be altered in an electronic medium. There is also no theoretical reason why functional prose should not and will not be organized in different ways for a quite different medium. Indeed, considering the implications for conventional literacy skills and concepts, some of which have been discussed above, it would seem only sensible to exploit the manipulative power of the new medium, to facilitate reader interaction with it and to provide opportunities not available to information gatherers until now.

Firstly, let us consider the presentation of conventional texts of a functional nature such as may be found in many subject textbooks. These often commence with an abstract followed by a linear argument or analysis. Traditionally, readers have then to scan the body of text to find the information they require. A computerized version of this resource material could be totally restructured in a branching format to allow readers the choice for divergence at any point of the original synopsis. They would then be able to follow any particular line of enquiry they wished to pursue. The format is particularly attractive technically because data organized in a hierarchical or tree structure expends fewest computing resources and in this sense allows very efficient retrieval. It would also be attractive to less fluent readers in that it would relieve them from addressing large passages of irrelevant information.

On the other hand, a typical frame of electronic print is a very small window through which to glimpse an electronic database. Users cannot glance around as in a newspaper nor flick through the pages as in a book. It is quite easy, therefore, for readers to lose their place in the hierarchical structure or never gain an overall appreciation of the structure of the information before them in the first place. In a book or newspaper, readers normally have some sense of where they are and can relate the part to the whole. They have some idea of the relationship between the page or article in front of them and the rest of the text. Increasingly, as users of electronic information retrieval systems move further along its branches, they lose any overall perspective which they may initially have had. The reader feels the need to map the information, however it is embodied. Conventional print media present a far more concrete opportunity for doing so. Electronic information storage and retrieval systems, by comparison, always appear opaque – abstract and intangible in overall form and structure to the information seeker.

Because of the restrictions placed upon the amount of print visible in any one frame, current electronic databases of this sort for home or school typically use a system of indexes, each one refining the subject chosen from the one before. This procedure might work well for the uninitiated; it can be tedious to the initiated. A proficient reader can become frustrated working through a long series of frames to elicit the information required, especially if it is not available at the end of the search. The proficient reader is one who repeatedly asks, 'Did I want to know this?' or, 'Is this new to me?'. The response to these questions prompts one of a number of reading strategies. If the answer to either question is negative the reader reacts by moving to another part of the text, quickly and efficiently. A branching interaction would not facilitate this strategy and the able reader could be left frustrated. The less fluent reader may gain from the direction and example afforded by a structured branching search of data (though he can also be easily distracted in his search and be diverted down an irrelevant branch). The more proficient reader can be left questioning whether he could not have obtained the information more efficiently in a conventional scanning exercise on a linear text. Moreover, the hierarchically organized data structure may be most inappropriate for the user who wishes to retrieve information that has multiple attributes.

Yet another issue is that a branching format ought to be carefully structured to allow it to be mapped onto the cognitive structures or patterns of thought and enquiry of the reader. This is an exceedingly difficult task in the first place and even if the structure of individual 'cognitive maps' does reveal that some hierarchical arrangements are more suitable than others, a database structured in this way is unlikely to be entirely satisfactory for every reader. Alternative ways of representing the information for users need to be considered.

With some hierarchically organized electronic databases progress has been made in overcoming problems associated with their use. One characteristic innovation has been the addition of a search facility in which users can type in key words to gain direct access to a relevant part of the database. Not only can this cut down 'access time' for an individual page but it can also facilitate jumps from one part of the tree to another. The idea of keywords can be taken further in a database comprising simply a collection of individual records. Here the keywords could be used to extract individual records and fields from files in a matching process.

A more loosely-structured database is a more flexible medium for readers. Here, however, the language and mode of interrogating the information stored (generative rather than selective) might necessitate the acquisition of new techniques, if not concepts. Although this design of information storage and transmission might be potentially very efficient, it does rely on the adoption of new literacy strategies which we cannot assume users of electronic text will necessarily develop on their own.

Indeed, electronic databases make considerable cognitive demands upon users. When information is stored in conventional textbooks and reference manuals, it can often be accessed (though not necessarily assimilated or efficiently extrapolated) using a very elementary reading strategy. Many readers who first learn a close reading strategy for fictional material then apply the same strategy to both fictional prose and reference material whatever their reasons for reading it. There is no obvious way to stop them doing so and although it might not be an efficient retrieval strategy, at least these information gatherers are able to access the data.

An electronic database is characteristically not accessible in the same way. The information is stored, retrieved and presented in a form which militates against the superimposition of a linear model on content or application of a close reading strategy, either or both of which readers may try to transfer from their encounters with conventional narrative prose. Furthermore, the interrogation of a database requires a user to formulate hypotheses and embody them in questions which are compatible with the structure of the database and the system of interrogation. Every user of such an information store is thus forced repeatedly to select and adopt the active, self-questioning reading strategies and other cognitive procedures which able reader/researchers adopt whenever they turn to conventional functional print resources. The implications for education are clear. Students must gain familiarity with electronic databases not just because of their increasing importance but also because of the modes of thinking they encourage. And students should do so in a purposeful educational context where they are encouraged towards personal enquiry and towards taking responsibility for their own learning.

Even for fluent readers the need for electronic information systems is vital. Since the days of Gutenberg, printed information has been doubling every fifteen years. In this century we realized its crisis proportions as its exponential growth became large enough to gain attention. The information explosion is already a problem for librarians and those in the forefront of information storage, processing and transfer. In the very near future, we shall all have to take account of vast quantities of knowledge. We cannot begin to assimilate it all. Rather we need means to store it, gain fast access to it and utilize it wisely. These are the prime strategies which information seekers need to acquire. On its own, the human brain is limited in its ability to acquire, store, process and output information. The new electronic medium should be seen therefore not as a gross mechanistic threat, but as a provider of the opportunity to extend, or at least to facilitate, our use of print for the storage, interpretation and transmission of information and experience.

Choices

In all this we must not shift our present emphasis. If communication is really to be facilitated, the emphasis still needs to be on human users rather than on machines. The poor quality of many electronic text displays is not necessarily an indication of the present state of the art of technological development. Sometimes it bears witness to the mismatch between the system of choices made available to the technical designers or to the choices they made and their knowledge of the psychology of human information processing. Sometimes it is simply their lack of willingness to implement such knowledge. Rather than concentrating on improving or attacking the technology, we should turn attention to human needs and capabilities in absorbing, processing and retrieving information. How do humans best transfer information from one mind to another? In this we need to know a great deal more about how the human brain processes information. In particular, we need to consider the factors involved in the comprehension and internalization of external data. Only then can we really choose the most efficient and satisfying means of communication.

Seen from this perspective, there ought to be no real challenge to our present literacy despite the fears which many of us have. Let us admit that for some purposes, in some situations, there might be more satisfying, more satisfactory, ways of representing and communicating information about our world than those we have traditionally employed. This will not be so in all cases. In years to come there may well arise strong economic, ecological, social, psychological or political arguments for a further transition from conventional to electronic print creation, storage, retrieval, manipulation and transmission. This is not to say that there ought to be a total substitution of electronic for paper technology. Some replacement has already taken place, particularly in commerce. Yet at the same time, this replacement has involved innovation in the way that information is represented and transmitted. Over time, it is quite likely that the new medium will develop its own characteristic stylistic conventions whenever textual information is stored and presented in electronic form. It is likely to be accompanied by its own literacy, even by its own verbal art form. Further substitution of electronic for conventional print would then be most inappropriate in some circumstances. For example, if our only access to books was electronic, there would be a distinct threat to that unique part of the experience which the reading of conventional books alone can offer. The electronic medium can and should replace paper print in some contexts for some purposes. At other times, it is cumbersome, uneconomic, psychologically unsuitable or stylistically unadaptable. Hard and soft copy, paper and screen, should be considered mutually complementary rather than mutually exclusive. The new medium is an extension of our present typographic communications media rather than a substitute for them.

Reading has always been a transaction at the heart of which is the act of converting arbitrary symbols into thoughts of things, people and actions. From its very origins, the reading/writing transaction has been humanizing. Writing was invented so that someone 'here' might record thoughts ('I count this many sheep.') and later feelings ('The Lord is my Shepherd.') so that someone 'there' might experience those thoughts and feelings at another time and place. The computerization of text is but an extension of that transaction. We humans, who alone read and write among all the creatures of which we know, have studied and cherished this transaction for so long that any major enhancement appears at first to be a threat. Nothing of value that we did before the advent of the computer ought to be lost. We must ensure that it cannot be. But that will only come about if we understand, appreciate and exploit the differences between the print media. It is vital that we begin to select and continue to identify the right medium for the right task. This is the most fundamental choice in this system of choices. Let us not be swayed purely or even primarily by economic, social or political arguments. Let us look at the nature of the material – its size, its subject, its characteristics, its life; let us look at the size and nature of the actual or intended audience or readership; let us consider, too, the use to be made of the material – its frequency, continuity, extent, precision and location. Then let us choose an appropriate method of storage, retrieval and presentation. Different matter will require different media. The future system of storage and access should be a mixed one. If we ensure that this happens, then the love, study and profit of reading will not only continue but it will flourish, extended and aided at times by a powerful new tool, itself an object of study.[2]

4 Talking, Listening and the Microcomputer

ANTHONY ADAMS

The role of talking and listening, of oracy, within the classroom presents teachers with a problem. On the one hand there would be universal agreement that the spoken word is important; on the other the problems of organizing classrooms specifically for the development of talk are considerable. Indeed, it could be said that the legitimization of talking and listening within the English curriculum, especially at secondary level, has been a problem for teachers ever since Wilkinson (then at the University of Birmingham in England) began to promote the concept of oracy in the early 1960s. Today, virtually all primary teachers and most secondary school teachers of English would accept in theory the importance of the spoken language in their work and in the language development of their students. This is especially so in view of the obvious, and now clearly recognized, role that talk plays in learning outside the school, especially in the home.

But, in practice, many teachers still find that classroom talk presents major management problems. Most recently, Lewis Knowles in *Encouraging Talk* (Methuen, 1983) explores some of the reasons for this:

> Teachers in secondary schools often find it difficult to involve their pupils in constructive classroom talk and the older the pupils get the greater the difficulty encountered. Added to this . . . is the fact that the present secondary curriculum insists on vast tracts of information being transferred from the teacher's head to those of his pupils: the kind of language use required for this purpose is of a different order from that envisaged in children's own speech. However, English teachers are fortunate in that their subject is not, by and large, dominated by 'content' . . . but is largely concerned with the development of language activity and skills through a wide variety of classroom materials. They are therefore better placed to plan situations where children can talk and, indeed, they have a professional responsibility to do so . . . One [strategy] which is being used increasingly in other areas of the curriculum as well as English is the small group discussion. This can be difficult to organize and control, particularly for the less experienced teacher, but allows all the class to join in and have their say in a discussion.[1]

Yet, in spite of the reluctance or fears of some teachers, talking and listening are firmly on the agenda in 1984. There are, for example, important shifts of emphasis being proposed in Scotland (discussed in more detail below) which will have the effect of firmly establishing the place of oracy within the new Scottish leaving certificate. This is already leading to the production of textbook materials to help teachers prepare their students for the new format examinations.[2] It is likely also that the new 16+ examinations in English south of the border may contain a substantial element of oral assessment. Some Examination Boards, such as the Oxford Delegacy, are already drawing up criteria for the assessment of group talk and discussion.

Problem-solving talk

With such developments in examination syllabuses the process of legitimization is now virtually complete. However, the practical classroom problems hinted at by Knowles and defined by Adams and Pearce in 1974 remain:

> Achieving [a] climate of group talk in the classroom requires that the children work in small groups, which can range from four to seven in number. The less experience the children have of group talk, the shorter the periods of time devoted to it have to be, and the more specific will be the task given each time. Much of the work will be done without the teacher's presence, since the teacher can be with only one group at a time. This can be an advantage, for the teacher needs to learn when to stand back and let a group get on with it. With several groups at work in the same room, of course, there will be a great deal of talk going on, and pupils need training and practice if they are to participate without interfering with the work of other groups ... Although group activity is normal enough in most junior schools, it is not often devoted to this most potent of all skills. For English ... group work should be as normal and natural a feature as field-work in geography or demonstrations in science.[3]

Elsewhere the same authors suggest that we are not very good at developing in students the skills of transactional and problem-solving talk, primarily because we do not give them sufficient practice in these activities. Ten years later, in 1984, it could certainly be cogently argued that we need to develop such skills even more urgently, that learning to work together in problem solving is an essential survival skill in (and for) present-day society. A few years ago one might have observed the way in which the telephone was taking primacy over written correspondence. Today the telephone may well be giving way to new developments in electronic mail: 'electronic chatter' is bringing together the spoken and written word in a totally novel way, and the implications of this for what we teach in schools have yet to be sorted out.

Many of the points made above in relation to talk have also been made in relation to the microcomputer. It has been frequently observed that to introduce a microcomputer into the classroom is also to introduce a major management problem. It, too, requires the provision of learning opportunities other than whole class teaching, and there are many reasons to prefer work at the computer to take place in groups, in size not unlike those recommended for group talk. It could well be that with the right programs, and the right patterns of classroom organization, the two sets of management problems will help to solve each other.

Common to the contributors to this book is the belief that we should aim at interactive programs rather than ones which encourage purely response from students. We see the most appropriate educational application of the computer as a stimulating aid to learning rather than as a teaching machine. The logistical problems of having one computer to some thirty students means that much of the work will necessarily have to go on in self-sustaining groups. Necessarily, too, the members of these groups will need to interact with each other; talking (and listening) has to go on. Moreover the talk has got to reach a clear and negotiated conclusion. Some member of the group has to type the next entry to the keyboard to move the program on to the next stage. At the lowest level the computer can provide both a stimulus and a focus for group decision making in the classroom. At a higher level, one of the continuing problems that teachers have with talk in the classroom is the difficulty of monitoring what has been going on in a group. How is it possible to determine to what extent the talk has been 'on target' and how successful it has been?

Clearly by such devices as recording screen activity on video-tape, or by elements in the programs themselves, it is possible for the teacher to inspect later the stages through which the group has passed in its quests for solutions to the problems or issues being explored.

We can see, therefore, an important role for the computer as a kind of neutral, non-threatening and non-censorious, silent Chair of a group, which provides a focus for the activity, keeps the group motivated, responds to whatever the group does, but also leaves its members free to make their own decisions, including mistakes.

Strictly speaking, of course, they are not making 'mistakes' but only decisions, the consequences of which have to be lived with. The advantage of working with a computer program is precisely that one can usually retrace one's own steps and try out, in different ways, the consequences of one's own thinking. In his early work on the use of adventure games in the English classroom, Chandler stressed this virtue of the microcomputer, and the opportunities for group talk and group decision making that such games provide.[4] This is even more true today with an increasing number of such games being developed specifically for educational purposes, including opportunities for students to make up their own adventures for other groups of students to explore.[5]

If the argument thus far is accepted, certain consequences will follow about the kinds of programs that are needed to make both talk and computers acceptable to teachers in the classroom. As with talk itself, 'much of the work will take place without the teacher's presence'. It follows, then, that the programs need to have qualities of robustness so that the enthusiasm of the group cannot crash them, and they need also to be free-standing, with enough on-screen prompts to enable the students to continue without needing to call for the teacher's assistance too frequently. An interesting minor feature of FACTFILE, one of the earliest products of the British government-sponsored Microelectronics Education Programme (MEP), was the introduction of an audible 'Help' signal which simply invited anyone, fellow students as well as a teacher, to go over to the group and to see what help was needed and could be given.

A case-study

It is now time to examine what some of this might look like in practice. First, as a kind of particularized case-study, Alastair McPhee of Strathclyde Regional Council describes at length some of the development work north of the border; interestingly enough, he, too, begins with the effects on the curriculum of changes in the examination system:

> One obstacle which has been placed in the path of those staff who have wished to proceed apace with the development of the oral skills of their students has been the fact that the examination system has hitherto devalued those skills at the expense of literacy skills, with which it feels very much more able to cope. Although CSE Mode 3 and SCOTBEC [the Scottish Business Education Council providing courses at 16+] have recently moved towards the inclusion of oral skills in their syllabuses, no national terminal examination in Scotland has involved them.
>
> The situation is, however, about to change with the implementation of the new Standard Grade Arrangements in 1986. Under these new arrangements, the skills of talk and listening will be examined at national level, and 40% of the assessment will depend upon them. This will in turn reflect an equal 25% balance in the English course amongst the four modes of talk, listening, writing and reading. In preparation for the new system, teachers have been busy over the past session or so in the development of oral skills. This development has taken place within school, and has been supported by Advisers and development officers. Nationally the Scottish Central Committee on English has been associated with the production of 'Hear-Say', a document which sets out to provide a rationale for oracy in the English classroom and to support it with exemplar materials.

Development groups working upon the production of software for microcomputers have been aware of the need for the materials they produce to include the recognition of the new place which oral skills will occupy in the English syllabus. They have found it difficult, however, to do this, partly because of unfamiliarity with the potential of the medium with which they are working, and partly because they appreciate that the skills of talk and listening depend upon sound, whereas the microcomputer appears to deal exclusively with literacy skills at its present stage of development.

Nevertheless, there has been some development in the area of oral work, and these groups have also been concerned to review materials produced for other purposes to see if they can be readily adapted to foster oral as well as written skills.

The following are some of the uses to which the microcomputer might be put in the teaching of oral skills. This list is by no means exhaustive: it simply represents a summation of the present state of development in this area. Without doubt there will be other new ways which will soon suggest themselves for the use of this increasingly impressive teaching tool. What is beyond doubt is that the micro will become an established feature of every school, eventually of every classroom, and that its charismatic qualities will be harnessed for an increasingly wide range of purposes across the curriculum and within each subject area. That implies that shortly micros *will* be used in the fostering of oral skills: what remains to be done is the development work which will see the creation of the software which teachers will need to achieve this. Our increasing awareness of the potential of the computer in learning will hasten this.

The first example of the association of the micro with the teaching of oral skills is in the adaptation of a by now fairly well-known program to provide an oral skills input into an existing 'writing only' programme of work. The tree-of-knowledge type of program, marketed variously as ANIMAL or CREATURES, lends itself well to such use. It also has the advantage of being exceedingly widely available in the schools. A project was prepared which invited the class to divide itself up into groups for purposes of research and investigation, using library texts and texts of imaginative literature. Each group was allocated one sub-topic within the general theme of 'Animals'. Examples of such topics were: 'Animals as Pets', 'Animals at Work', 'Animals in Zoos', and so on. The project was so structured that each group would complete its assignments on each sub-topic, and then move on to another: the sub-topics were thus spread evenly around the class. Although it is true to say that the class by dint of the very fact that they were working collaboratively in small groups were involved in discussion and in linking their talk to writing (both valuable activities in themselves), it was felt that a session in which talk skills could be more accurately structured under the guidance of the teacher would be valuable. Such a session would also enable observational assessment of the talk skills of the pupils to be made.

Thus, one of the sub-topics was to be the use of the CREATURES program in its version by Daniel Chandler. A microsystem was made available in a corner of the classroom: this was valuable as it enabled a check to be made on other classroom activity – a check which would not have been possible had the computer been centrally located away from the main learning locus. More subtly, perhaps, it also served to establish the legitimate place of the computer in the learning process – not as a novelty or as an expensive device for the playing of games, but as a substantive part of the classroom scene. The children then operated the program in their groups as and when their turn arose, 'teaching' the computer their own animals, and framing the all important questions distinguishing their own creatures from those which the machine already 'knew'. Once again it is important to note that the interactive process was not merely that of pupil to machine, as is the case with much commercially available material, but a complex one involving the group dynamic as well as that of the computer. The overall assessment of those teachers who used the program in this way was that pupils became actively stimulated to talk, and that the talk resulting from the use of the machine was purposeful.

A second example of the use of the computer is that where material produced for use in other subjects has been modified by teachers of English to take account of the need to stimulate talk activities. The Scottish Microelectronics Development Programme has produced an excellent simulation entitled THE PRINTON BYPASS. This program was actually produced for use in Social Studies classes but, as will be seen, it is eminently suitable for adaptation for use in the teaching of English. The simulation is that of a road bypass being constructed around the town of Printon. As would be expected from a program developed for use in the Schools Traffic Education Programme, the original objectives were those of heightening awareness as to the planning issues involved. Hence the program provides information on materials, costs, and other parameters of road construction. But it also involves people – and choices. There are three routes involved, each of which raises different planning issues. It does not need a very great deal of imagination on the part of the teacher to realise the potential of this. Chairmen of Planning Committees can be appointed. Such people have to make speeches, address public meetings. Discussions have to be held to decide the best location of the road. Pressure groups hold counter meetings, individuals protest violently, politicians, local and national, can attempt mollification. All these activities involve *talk*. Of course, the actual talk itself takes place off-computer: but is that not true of life itself? The point seems to be that the computer is used to drive the talk, to generate it. The talk itself takes place in whatever context is most appropriate – taped assignment, drama, interview, or whatever.

This use of an existing program for modification to the needs of the English classroom and the teaching of talk is an interim stage before what seems to be at present the latest stage of development – although the situation changes so quickly that new materials may well be to hand or in progress as this is written. That situation is the construction of a program which is deliberately designed from the outset to foster English activities in this mode. PROJECT SPACE, shortly to be released by the Scottish Microelectronics Development Programme, is an example of such a program. Briefly, each group in the classroom is the crew of a space cruiser, and the program consists of the presentation of certain assignments on the VDU in linear sequence which constitute the voyage through space and the eventual achievement of the mission. Certain of the assignments are talk assignments: for example, students are required to act and/or tape the scene on board the space cruiser when the enemy vessel is sighted. This requires the quite advanced talk skills of simulating different reactions to an unknown situation, and involves students in a collaborative exercise. An example of a more individualised talk activity, involving a different purpose for talk, is when the notorious space pirate, Konlee, has to be interrogated by the victorious crew. This is suggested as pair work with students having the opportunity to rehearse interview skills in a highly structured situation. Likewise the communication messages (cloze and sequencing exercises) demand group discussion for their successful completion. Thus the project sets out deliberately to energise three distinctly different talk situations in the classroom through the ability of the micro to create a fantasy on its screen.

It would not do to complete this account without some reference to the receptive mode counterpart to talk – listening. Although a microcomputer can create listening situations through the use of its SOUND capability, its repertoire is, to say the least, somewhat limited – though the advent of the speech synthesiser is an exciting prospect. However, it is possible to create the situation through the micro where the student is enabled, or persuaded, to carry out listening in a situation provided by the software. Thus, in PRO-JECT SPACE, for example, the students' first assignment is to receive their instructions for the mission from a tape-recorded message from Mission Control which is provided as part of the kit. The groups then return to the computer for a 'Flight Check' which is, in fact, an aural comprehension based upon the information received from the tape. Other programs currently under development as part of the preparation for the implementation of Standard Grade with its focus on a four-mode model of English teaching use taped material similarly as part of a kit, the assignments being generated as part of a context provided by the computer. It can, of course, also be argued that group discussion of itself generates listening as part of the process.

It is to be hoped that development of software which encourages oral skills development will continue at a pace which will meet the demands of teachers who wish to bring their classrooms into the age of microtechnology, and who wish to do so in a way which is creative and inventive.

McPhee's hopes are borne out by developments south of the border. There are a number of teacher groups in different Local Education Authorities working along similar lines to those that he describes. A new software company, CLASS (Cambridge Language Arts Software Services), has been formed which seeks to enable precisely this kind of work by teachers.[6] One of its first programs, SPACE PROGRAMME ALPHA, bears a strong family resemblance to the PROJECT SPACE program that McPhee describes. It is essentially an extended role-play exercise played in groups by pupils in which the roles are randomly assigned by the computer. Throughout the simulation, which provides plenty of occasions for talk in itself as well as work in the other language modes, the groups have to keep a 'Captain's Log', which is, of course, kept on tape. Since the whole simulation has been devised by practising teachers and has been worked out in their own classrooms, the problems of managing both talk and computers that have been discussed above have been uppermost in their minds. The published materials will, in fact, contain a detailed set of lesson plans so as to show by means of a matrix how the various groups can move through the activities available to them without getting in each other's way.

This seems very important. If some teachers are still uncertain about how to handle talk in the classroom, others are even more so about how to handle computers. If we want to build up expertise and willingness to experiment in both these fields it is essential to provide materials that will generate sufficient confidence in teachers to actually employ them. CLASS has gone still further than this; one of its earliest published programs has deliberately been designed with the beginning teacher in mind so far as the use of computers is concerned. The actual computer program, though interesting, is only one relatively small element within the total suite of materials, which are designed so as to stimulate language work across all four modes with particular attention to group talk.

Such thinking, in terms of suites of mutually supporting materials, is becoming more common amongst software publishers, as in many of the excellent simulations being produced by Ginn in Britain. As in much else that has been discussed in this chapter, there is a close analogy between the use of computers in the classroom and the use of talk. Talking and listening, as two of the language modes, cannot themselves be seen as 'freestanding' – they have to have a constant interplay with reading and writing as well. Certainly we need to see more use of talk in the classroom but as part of a total orchestration of language activities.

This is why, although in the inevitable arrangement of a book such as this 'writing' appears as a separate topic, we must not ignore here the vital relationship between talk and writing. Britton's phrase 'Writing floats on a sea of talk' is by now well known, and is generally thought of as indicating the importance of the 'pre-writing' stage in composition and the role that talk plays in it. If students can engage, however, in the more public activity of screen-writing, especially with the new opportunities for several inputs into the computer such as is provided by the development of new keyboards, such as Quinkey, the possibilities of enabling the continuous role of talk and the exchange of ideas during the composition process becomes all the more interesting. The talk interaction within the group can continually be transferred to the text on which it is working as they experiment with the text they are creating on the screen. The one will regularly reinforce the other.

All this is so relatively new that we do not know much about the effects of such collaborative writing, or about the kind of talk that it will generate in the classroom. At the Department of Education in the University of Cambridge, research has begun to investigate this; preliminary observations suggest that both the talk and the writing are enhanced by working in this way. The finished product, of course, gives the teacher an opportunity of monitoring the kind of activities that have been going on in the group. So far as the talk is concerned the sampling of the process through which the product has been achieved is much more difficult to accomplish. Such experiments in collaborative writing and talking provide a further example, however, of the way in which the microcomputer can act as a focus for group activity without the teacher needing to be present so as to free both students and teachers for other encounters.

DEVELOPING TRAY

So far as we have been discussing the role of the microcomputer as the silent neutral chair of a group discussion together with its role in the development of collaborative talk. There are, however, numerous other functions that talk can perform. Certainly in many real-life situations there is often a competitive element to talk. A particular development of this, which the micro makes possible, is seen when the computer becomes a competitor within the group. McPhee describes above the experience of 'teaching' the micro in his variation of use of the CREATURES program; another well-known program in wide circulation is Bob Moy's DEVELOPING TRAY (see Appendix 2 for details). In this, a group of students has to interpret the likely letter equivalents to a series of dashes on the screen, indicating the letters in a text for which the punctuation is also supplied. This calls upon all the resources of the group in thinking about such issues as letter frequency, collocation, style, and semantic clues. It works, in practice, as a kind of total 'cloze' exercise.

Anyone who has used this program, either with students or with adults, will be only too well aware of the immense power the program has to generate discussion. The only disadvantage it has when used as a demonstration program for in-service work is the impossibility of getting the group away from the program until they have cracked the code and 'developed' the text. In the version that is most generally available there is a built-in on-screen scoring system so that the group is penalized for mistaken predictions or for asking for undue help. By contrast, it is rewarded for making intelligent predictions about the likely occurrence of letters.

Using this program is highly revealing for the way in which it is capable of stimulating both productive talk and a productive style of working in the group. Most groups begin with wild guesses but rapidly realize that they are giving away large numbers of points in consequence. They, therefore, have to learn to talk through the problem posed, to work out what might be the most intelligent solution to the problem. This leads to the development of much more mature strategies. The point here is that the talk is generated in the process of working out the solution and is effectively stimulated by working against the computer program in a competitive mode. It would, of course, be possible to use the stimulus found in many arcade games of recording the 'best score to date' so that later groups could try to beat their predecessors while working on the same material. This would seem both unnecessary and undesirable in practice; sufficient stimulus is provided by the sense of competition between the group and the computer which rapidly develops.

The net effect of this is to transform what is essentially a linguistic and intellectual exercise into a kind of 'game' – a more literary version of playing a game such as chess or bridge against the computer.

Another way to implement the program is to have a teacher, who knows the text, working alongside the group, who does the actual keying in of the group's answers, stimulating their talk in the process by stretching their ability to predict possible combinations of letters. In this case the teacher is able to move the group forward faster than it would otherwise be able to go and is able, by careful questioning, though not by direct prompting, to extend the thinking of the group. It is not at all unlike the exercises in group cloze or group prediction described and developed by Christopher Walker in 1974 but rather easier to organize and control. This application of DEVELOPING TRAY has been carried out with quite large, even class-sized groups; all that is necessary is an appropriately sized screen for display of the material.

It is interesting how different the actual teaching experience is in using DEVELOPING TRAY in the two ways described. Both produce a good deal of talk but the talk is quite different in the teacher-led and the non-teacher-led group. Again more research is needed in areas such as this. It would be interesting to record both kinds of groups working with the same basic material and to compare the strategies employed in both cases.

There are a number of other programs being devised which put the students in the position of being a competitor against the machine. Most 'real time' programs are necessarily of this kind. In Britain, for example, the software company Five Ways has produced a program in which a journey across Europe has to be negotiated against the clock and where timetables and reserves of currency have to be manipulated. In its present form it would seem difficult to use it with a group: the decisions have to be made too quickly to allow for much real discussion. But it might be possible to build in a facility for 'stopping the clock' which would allow the discussion to run its course before the decision of the group is entered without losing the competitive effect and stimulus of the 'real time' application.

If the scoring system is removed there is the possibility of a yet different role for the computer, that of challenger, where a problem is posed to which the group has to find the answer. Perhaps the simplest illustration of this would be where the computer has 'thought of' a random number between 1 and (say) 1000 and the group has to 'guess' what the number is. Again experience of working with groups with programs of this kind shows how quickly there is a development both of cohesiveness within the group and of intellectually coherent problem-solving strategies.

Asking questions

As this is being written the recent work of Lunzer and Gardner has seen publication in the shape of *Learning from the Written Word* (Oliver and Boyd, 1984). This is essentially concerned with developing students' skills in coping with text as a means of imparting information and makes extensive use of techniques of 'modelling' in relation to text: producing tables, labelling diagrams and the like. The authors are strongly of the view that such work is best done by students talking in groups to solve the conceptual problems that are being posed. There seems every possibility here for a greater inter-relation between reading, talking and the use of computers. The possibilities for modelling exercises opened up by the easy availability of computer graphics through utility programs are potentially enormous. CLASS, for example, has in active preparation a note-making program of such a kind that will enable students to develop their own personally designed databases in relation to the texts that they are studying. Although the program is initially being designed for private study there would be every advantage if such a program were to be used in groups.

Several English teachers have already experimented with the use of student-designed databases using the programming language PROLOG. This makes use of logic programming in which the description of what is being entered has to be clearly and precisely stated. By its means databases can be easily set up and then interrogated, edited and amended. One teacher describes the role of the computer here as being rather like that of secretary to the group:

> It allowed the pupils to move easily between specific details and generalized rules which they could test by example. It would therefore appear to be a useful tool in this kind of discussion and a valuable aid to clearer thinking. The computer can often slow down the rush of ideas, give time for reflection and take away the notion of adversarial combat from debate . . . This sort of computer use has . . . to do with working together, teamwork, co-

operation and problem solving to attempt a solution to a question. This may well be of value to [students'] future working situation.[7]

Elsewhere Brent Robinson has written of his work using PROLOG in the teaching of literature for the illumination of the structure and relationships of characters in a play such as Shakespeare's *Macbeth*. In the same paper he describes students working in groups on a 'mystery' program in which a murder had to be solved:

> The computer was loaded with the database though its actual contents were not revealed to the pupils and its listing forbidden at all times. Instead, the pupils were provided with duplicated sheets on which . . . relationships and specimen questions were written. The pupils were divided into groups and asked to solve a murder by deduction and interrogation of the computer. Each group then discussed the subject, formulating hypotheses and translating them into SIMPLE PROLOG questions to key into the computer. Here they were helped in their thought processes by the logical nature of PROLOG itself. When an interrogative had been formulated, one member of the group went off to query the computer. There being only one computer between the thirty-four pupils in the room, a pupil might be absent for four to five minutes waiting . . . to take his turn at the keyboard. In his absence, the rest of the group assumed the hypothesis to be correct and worked on this assumption. His return either made the group retrace their discussion – a useful exercise in itself – or added support to their deductions.

Robinson reported finding students able to sustain discussion of this kind for a full hour and goes on to describe the written, and other oral, activities that resulted from the discussion. Here is clearly a relatively new and powerful tool for the English teacher in a language that has the advantage that its structure is in many ways very similar to that of English itself.

Persuasive and conversational talk

We have been concentrating so far mainly on collaborative talk and variations of problem-solving talk. It may well be that this is what computers are most likely to encourage. But there are, of course, many other aspects of talk that need consideration in the English classroom, persuasive and conversational talk being prominent amongst them. McPhee has suggested how, by using the computer to 'drive' the talk, opportunities can be taken for persuasive talk. The opportunity given to the teacher of enabling group talk in a controlled, but non-teacher directed, environment should make it more possible to find time for the development of conversational talk in the classroom.

So far as this last element is concerned micros may have (as so often) both advantages and disadvantages. Stephen Marcus has written of the dangers of the 'host in the machine' and there is evidence of students who regard their computer as their 'best friend'. Worries were expressed by some at the 1984 NATE Conference about students who spent their time interacting with a machine and found it increasingly difficult to establish relationships with people, who are so much more unpredictable than computers! This is one reason why so much stress has been laid throughout this chapter on the importance of group work. There is no doubt that the danger of computer use having an anti-social effect on some users is an aspect of the microcomputer revolution about which teachers need to be on their guard. It is, in fact, a feature of that revolution that schools will need increasingly to become places in which pupil-to-pupil and pupil-to-teacher interaction takes place. If they remain merely places for information transmission the need for schools may well disappear altogether. The point has been well put by Dale Shuttleworth who was responsible for setting up a system of alternative schools for the Toronto Board of Education, writing in the *Times Educational Supplement* on 2 October 1981:

> Unless we change our schools, we shall soon be bypassed. IBM and Westinghouse have plenty of programs coming along to 'educate' kids. The 'content' side of education can be provided on videotape and by computer. If the schools don't change, less and less money will be voted to the state school system and commercial interests . . . will dominate the education of the future. Until teachers realise that they have to become masters of process – how you learn, how you relate to others – and are seen to be expert in this, a takeover of education by big business will remain a danger.

However, provided we keep this caveat in mind, there may well be certain cases where the micro has a particular role to play so far as the development of talk in some individual children is concerned. All teachers are familiar with the shy or reticent child whom it is exceedingly difficult to draw out in class. It may be that such a student is likely to feel less threatened by a 'machine' than by a human teacher: we already know from clinical experience of some evidence of patients responding more honestly and easily to a computer taking a case history than to a family doctor. How to handle this and, at the same time, ensure that such a student does not become 'machine dependent' seems a matter for skilled teaching of the kind that no microcomputer will ever be able to replace.

We did hear, however, at the 1984 NATE Conference interesting accounts by a teacher dealing with pupils with special needs. She found problems in the classroom with phobics who refused to talk with maladjusted children who insisted on talking about all the wrong things at the wrong time. In both cases her experience was that the introduction of the computer into the classroom had proved a considerable help. It led to the stimulation of controlled and productive talk between students, and with the teacher, even if they were only talking about the games that they played with the computer and with the ones they had at home.

Similarly with physically handicapped students there is already a good deal of evidence that the use of special keyboards can help them overcome their disabilities. If we take account of the interaction between talking, writing and reading that has been discussed above, there seem to be a number of ways in which microcomputers in the classroom can help develop the potential of those suffering from specific, and even multiple, handicaps. In the light of the implications of the prevailing philosophy of the increasing presentation of handicapped students in mainstream education this becomes a matter of considerable importance. There are practical difficulties created by this well-intentioned legislation, yet computer-assisted learning may provide a way forward. It can encourage students to help each other, and it can allow the handicapped to take as full a part as possible, for example, in discussion of a situation presented on-screen.

Questions such as those raised above about the relationship between the individual student and the microcomputer relate also to the important question of where exactly the micro should be situated in the school, at least as long as it remains a relatively scarce resource.

There are certainly strong arguments for basing the computer in the library resources area, if one exists, so that it is easily accessible to all and is regarded as a reference tool in the same way as other resources in the library. In schools that are open-plan in design, or that have a style of 'open concept' teaching (such as many British primary or middle schools), there is much to be said for this. On the other hand, there is also much to be said, as McPhee suggests, for the computer forming part of the natural talking and learning environment of the classroom. Certainly, if we take the role of talking and listening in schools seriously, we shall want to create areas in our schools and classrooms where children can just sit and talk or discuss quietly. There is no reason why an area in association with the library should not be adapted for this purpose. It might be as well to ensure that this was also the kind of area in which a computer is placed so as to facilitate students trying things out as and when they think of them. It remains the case that many schools have been built to create environments that are effectively hostile to the development of talk amongst students. The attempt to solve some of the managerial problems created by the positioning of the micro needs to be looked at in relation to the overall design of the school if we are persuaded that the primary use of micros in English classes should be their use in groups for the stimulation, monitoring and enhancement of group discussion.

A focus for talk

Necessarily this chapter has only dealt with some limited areas of a highly complex subject. It would be a great mistake to imagine that microcom-

puters will solve all our problems with talking and listening in the classroom. There will remain many areas where only the teacher (and other
students) are likely to be of help. It is unlikely that, in any real sense, micros will have much to contribute directly in the area of inter-personal
relationships in spite of the seductive appearance of many artificial intelligence programs. But enough has been said to suggest that they do have
an important role to play and that they can effectively provide opportunities for teacher disengagement so that more time is freed for more
personal engagement with students.

We already know that such activities as the making of an audio-tape
recording helps to keep students 'on task' in non-teacher directed talk.
They have a sense of achievement in the work on which they are engaged.
The same seems to be true of the introduction of a computerized task into
a group. The presence of the computer seems to give a sense of 'status' to
the task and therefore provides a focus for the work of the student group.
If it can go further than this and extend the work of the group beyond their
immediate involvement with the computerized task so as to 'drive the
talk', in McPhee's telling phrase, the micro will have made a distinctive
contribution to a still contentious and difficult area of the English curriculum.

5 Evaluating Computer Programs

DIANA THOMSON

When considering the microcomputer as a learning aid for purposes other than programming, one may say that the computer is only as useful as the software that is run on it. In the area of literacy skills, or the Language Arts as they are known in the US, many computer programs are now becoming commercially available. Whether or not they are useful to individual teachers and students is another matter. Whether or not they live up to their producer's claims is still another.

The teacher's role as evaluator of such programs cannot be underestimated. Time spent on evaluating software will not only allow a teacher to become familiar with a range of computer capabilities, but the insight thus gained will put teachers in a position to demand more and better software from the producers. In the long run, a steady exposure to software will make teachers, as an interest group, more eager to take an active role in the decisions that go into the design of software. It may be that this is the only way in which teachers will get what they want and need from the computers in their schools.

How then should one proceed? The very first step is to make sure that software is available for viewing. Some local education authorities are able to buy software for demonstration at courses so that their teachers can view before buying. Some publishers may be persuaded to donate free samples to a local resource centre. In Britain this might be a teachers' centre or a county educational computing centre. In the US it could be a university's curriculum library, a teacher resource centre, or the school district office in a large city or county. Teachers cannot expect producers to send out samples to individual schools: far too many teachers violate the producers' copyright and the best software is often produced by small houses which barely have an advertising budget. Nor can we wait until *all* teachers have become informed and experienced evaluators; the most effective strategy at present seems to be for interested teachers to get together with their local computing and subject advisers to form an evaluation team.

The first major step in coming to terms with computers is the realization that to be a good judge of software it is not necessary to be able to program the computer. There are plenty of people who can do this efficiently; indeed many children achieve competence in programming the computer to do what is required. These people may, or may not, produce an adequate piece of educational software. It is up to teachers to inform them whether they have succeeded, and not be hoodwinked by programmers into believing that all programs are educationally valuable.

Once teachers have become more familiar with software, they are in the position to offer workable ideas and suggestions to programmers. This is not to say that ideas and suggestions should not be made prior to this, but offered from a position of understanding and backed by hard facts, ideas and suggestions are more persuasive than gut reactions, even though the outcome may be the same.

So, how can the 'average' non-technical teacher achieve competence in assessing software? Firstly, it is necessary to look at the types and styles of software currently in use, whether or not it is in the assessor's own discipline. Some of the problems with software design are often more readily apparent when you are dealing with subject matter in which you are not an 'expert'. If you are feeling a little inadequate to the learning task, your experience in using the computer will be closer to that of your students in your own discipline, who are struggling not only with the software *per se* but with the subject matter. Software should protect the student from unnecessary uncertainty and difficulty.

In this chapter references to software are not confined to the Language Arts: one of the interesting effects of the arrival of the computer is the way in which it often seems to lead to a renewal of interest amongst teachers in 'language across the curriculum', particularly since software for group use can often be an extraordinary generator of purposeful talk.

Familiarization can be achieved both through 'hands-on' experience and reading. In all assessments, it is essential to take into account the problems of using a microcomputer in the classroom. One computer shared among thirty students requires a different type of software, or different classroom organization, from the provision of one computer for ten students. Software should be adaptable as provision increases and should not become redundant as a result of increased availability of computer time. With proper care, a good purchase should last a few years at least.

What are the basic requirements of good software? These factors should be independent of the style and type of programs. I will consider the requirements under five main headings: Technical Aspects, Presentation, The 'User Interface', Modes of Use, and Educational Content.

Technical aspects

Professor Tom Stonier of Bradford University has described three stages in the development of educational software:

1 *Circa 1970:* Where there was any educational software at all, it tended to be drill and practice type programs produced by programmers with little knowledge of educational process.
2 *Circa 1978:* Programs produced by teachers which were more interesting and had a clear educational objective. The programs were, however, not robust and could easily be crashed by the 'negative creativity' of some children or 'computer illiterate' teachers. These programs were best used by the authors only.
3 *Now:* Programs are being written by teachers who have become better programmers, or by professional programmers and graphics designers directed by educators. The programs are often individually excellent, but *ad hoc*, and have not been placed in, nor designed for, a structured curriculum.

It is a sad fact that in the eyes of many teachers, many commercial software houses have only advanced to stage 2 in Professor Stonier's list. In addition, there are numerous, small 'one-man' software houses, whose programs are cheap, and available by mail-order, whose limit is also stage 2 at best. Whilst many programs are good value, the slick graphics and high sounding ideals can easily deceive the unwary.

The first stage of any evaluation should be the ease of loading the program into the computer. Whilst it is certainly possible for worthwhile use to be made of cassettes as a storage medium, novices can be easily discouraged by the slow and unreliable loading of programs on cassettes. Disc-drives are expensive, but they are far faster and more reliable, and their greater flexibility can lead to far more powerful programs than cassette-based ones. Some British schools may not be able to afford them, but disc-drives are strongly recommended, especially for use in the Language Arts, and local education authorities should be urged to support their acquisition.

A factor, at present relatively unimportant, but which will become important in future, is the ability of software to run on a network. Very few programs give any indication of whether this is a possibility, and it is definitely worth enquiring, if only to encourage manufacturers to label their products. Network compatability is a plus, but lack of it cannot be considered a minus unless it has to run on a network now or in the very near future.

Technically the excellence of a program should be unquestionable. A wrong answer, a mispressed key or a heavy hand should not upset the program, neither should the mischievous input of a 'show-off'. If the program is to be used with primary or lower-secondary students, robustness during input of data is essential. Older, well-motivated students will usually be all right with less rigid criteria of technical robustness, but it is always better to be safe.

To check for these attributes, the best policy is to feign ignorance. Does the program 'crash' when you press some unexpected keys? If you are using a program on a BBC computer, for instance, at any point when a keyboard input is required try the following:

1 Does the cursor change or move unexpectedly when an arrow key is pressed?
2 Hold down CTRL and press L. Does the screen blank out?
3 Press ESCAPE. Does a message appear such as 'Escape at line 1000' or does the program respond appropriately.

Annoying problems can also occur on first running the program. There are children with names of more than 10 letters (Christopher is a common example). Often inputs of this length cannot be made, and it is annoying to the child. Young children should not have to deal with upper- and lower-case letters, CAPS LOCK and SHIFT LOCK.

If a program requires a YES/NO or Y/N response, it should not proceed if any other key is depressed. A numeric response should not accept letters; an alphabetic response should not accept numbers; words should not be split across lines and scrolling of the screen display is usually unnecessary.

It is easy to carry out such simple tests and a program that fails too frequently can be rejected on these criteria.

Untidy screen-displays are all too often indicative of a poorly thought out and ill-tested program.

Few programs will match up to all technical requirements, and regrettably teachers will have to accept the current situation. There is no reason, however, for not expecting and demanding the highest standards in the future.

Presentation

In checking the technical aspect, the presentation of the program also becomes obvious. This is best divided into sub-sections:

Text
Graphics
Sound
Documentation

Character size

Large-size text characters are often desirable for young children. It is also useful for concentrating action and attention on a particular aspect of the program or position on the screen. At the same time it is worth mentioning that correct symbols for divide and multiply, instead of / and *, should be provided. Correct case is also essential.

Density of text

A screen full of information is daunting. Presented paragraph by paragraph, or sentence by sentence, and well spaced, the same information becomes more palatable.

Colour

Colour is a useful tool: used to advantage it can attract and direct the eye; used to excess it can confuse. Consistency of colours throughout a program makes it easy on the eye and facilitates usage, especially if prompts are given in a constant colour. Flashing colours can attract, but children quickly become tired of too much. If it irritates at the start, it will certainly annoy before long. Children may be confronted with flashing colours for far longer than the assessor of the program.

Timing

What is easily read by an adult may not be so by a child, so delays in the presentation of sequential text may be advantageous. However, boredom quickly sets in if the delays are too long; a good program is one that can be paced by a child, by pressing the SPACE BAR for example. Fuller explanations should be available on paper.

Language

Language must be appropriate to the student. This is obvious to any teacher, but confronted by a program with other points to check, it is easily forgotten. Unless a 'concept keyboard' (a programmable pressure pad) is used, children quickly develop the language necessary to handle a computer program. RETURN (ENTER), DELETE and SPACE BAR should prove no difficulty especially if the program is consistent in its approach. (RETURN after entering information, SPACE BAR to continue, etc.) The difficulty comes in matching the level of language with the complexity of the program. For example, a simple typing exercise does not need a page of complicated instructions. It may seem risible, but there are many programs in which this type of problem is apparent. If such a program requires that help should be given to the child to understand the operation of the program, then that help should be confined to the teacher's pages or the documentation.

Another language problem becomes evident: that of language for use in programs for remedial work. It has taken some time to realize that the subject matter of infant readers is unsuitable for 14-year-old slow learners, who can play computer games even if they cannot compute or read, and it should not be forgotten in the context of computer programs. Fourteen-year-olds do not like to be patronized.

Sound

Sound may be a novelty in some computer programs: it is a necessity in most music programs. It can be a curse in the classroom, especially if the machine is used for individual or group work whilst the remainder of the class have their own tasks. It should be possible to turn the sound off easily, without recourse to the listing, unless it is essential. There are some programs in which the use of sound can be misleading, giving rise to wrong concepts.

Graphics

The judgement of this is best left to the individual teacher's discretion. Graphics should satisfy the eye. If graphs and charts are used, it is sensible to check that the scales are suitable and that they are truly representative of the information. Teachers unused to the way such graphical representations can distort figures and in awe of computer-generated data may be easily fooled.

Colour and degree of resolution in graphics are often a function of available memory and this varies among machines. High-resolution graphics come close to real drawings whilst low-resolution graphics give pictures made of small blocks. It is unfair to criticize a program's graphics when memory is the limiting factor. The teacher must judge whether the graphics are appropriate.

Documentation

Good documentation should comprise three parts:

1 an outline of the program's aims,
2 a sketch of the suggested method of use, and
3 a blow-by-blow account of the mechanism of its use.

The first can obviously help sales of the program, but even so, it is surprising how many programs lack an adequate description of their aims. The second is not an essential part of the documentation, but is certainly desirable. Confidence on the part of the teacher in using a particular piece of software is gained more quickly if the initial planning of classroom organization, philosophy of usage and suggested place in the syllabus are detailed in the first place. The teacher then has the confidence to criticize, adapt and replan an approach to fit the needs of the class. Such an approach has been considered 'lazy teaching', but to the harassed teachers of the present day, with all the other pressing claims on their time, it is probably a quicker way of reaching personal competence and improved student response than many others. From personal experience it has been found that such an approach brings beneficial and unexpected results.

The third part of the documentation, that of a complete description, key-press by key-press, should always be provided, if only to satisfy the old adage 'If all else fails read the instructions'. Lengthy technical details are not needed, but the designer's suggestions should be supplied.

Many simple programs for children contain sufficient documentation within the program itself. If this is the case, the instructions should be clear and, ideally, easily accessible from any point within the program. Few programs match up to these standards.

Very clear instructions on altering programs to suit different kinds of printers should always be given.

Poor documentation should not, however, deter the teacher from purchasing a good program. It is then up to the teacher to provide the necessary notes.

The 'user interface'

In applying the previous criteria to software, it should quickly become obvious to the evaluator that there are various ways in which a program can be driven by the user. In evaluation it is beneficial to understand these methods as they can often determine whether a program can be useful with a particular group or age range of children, or with a certain computer/child ratio.

One technical term for the way in which the student interacts with the program is 'the user interface' (other terms are 'the front end' or the 'drive system') there are four main styles in use. Most software houses may use any style which is appropriate to the particular piece of software and may use combinations of styles; others can be more rigid and keep to the same style.

Menu-driven

In this mode the options open to the user are presented in the form of a list or menu, numbered, lettered, or highlighted. The choice is then made by pressing the appropriate number or letter, or moving the highlight using appropriate keys and pressing RETURN when the choice is featured. At these points a single key entry is all that is required, and it would be pleasant to think that menus could be standardized on numbers as numbers are easier to find on a keyboard. A standard way of returning to the menu page should be by pressing the ESCAPE key at any point in the program.

Command structure

This mode of use pioneered in England by the Advisory Unit for Computer Based Education (AUCBE) at Hatfield, and consists of various commands that can be entered when a colon (:) appears on the screen. Many commands are common to many programs; some are specific to one, but for any particular program none need be learned. Typing COMMANDS in response to : gives a list of all the commands, and HELP followed by any command will give more information about that particular command. The actual commands depend on the nature of the program, for example, a 'turtle' graphics program would have commands like FORWARD, LEFT and RIGHT. Commands can often be abbreviated to the first few letters, and the use of 'function keys' to represent commands for the BBC machine has alleviated some problems with careless spelling. Function keys are special keys which can be programmed in software to perform particular functions. Needless to say command structure is difficult to use at first, even by highly intelligent adults, but it does have the advantage that, once mastered, all programs using the same technique become easy to drive. It certainly does come into its own with programs such as DART (a turtle graphics program) and QUERY/QUEST (a database program). Programs using command structure should be practised by the teacher before use with a class and are not suitable for very young children for whom typing is a problem.

Single-key commands

This mode could perhaps be called 'son of command structure', and is best explained by use of an example. One of the British MEP's Micro-primer programs is EUREKA, a program which aims to teach aspects of graphical interpretation. A graph of water-level against time is plotted, reflecting the actions of a man having a bath. The sequence of operations is controlled by single keys, T for taps on/off, P for plug in/out, H for Help etc. The keys are obvious once the program has been run. This mode of use is easier for young children.

Single path

A program which allows only one path through it has a single path structure. The rate of progression through the program should be under the user's control throughout. This method is found in simple programs.

From these brief descriptions, it is obvious that some 'driving methods' are indeed more suitable for young children or less experienced teachers.

Having covered all these methods, the mode of use within the classroom
is the next area to consider.

Modes of use

Some programs are designed to use the computer as an electronic
blackboard. It is clearly a valuable mode of use, but limited if the class is
large and the monitor or TV is small. A notable example of this type of
program is WRITING, by Anita Straker. A lower-case letter is chosen by
the teacher and it is drawn carefully on the screen, showing the movement
of the pencil, until a new letter is chosen or the program terminated. This
is an invaluable aid to the infant teacher as individual help can be given
with a quick look at the screen. Other teaching programs by the same
author use this mode also. Typically, she uses large letters and figures and
very clear diagrams. An electronic blackboard program that uses very
small letters for anything other than initial instructions to the teacher or
teacher prompts, should be scrutinized carefully.

Individual learning programs are the most common variety of educational software. Every software house has its own example and it is this
style of program that is mainly available to the home market under the
heading 'educational'. In British schools, the older term for such programs was 'drill and practice'; respectability has been attempted by changing the name to 'structured learning'. No matter – the method of learning
is well tried and tested, it is only the approach that is new. The same
judgement should be applied to the new as well as the old.

A teacher who tried to teach spelling simply by administering spelling
tests would quickly be condemned. Similarly a program that gives no correction of wrong answers, nor instructions as to how a correct answer can
be achieved, should be viewed with scepticism. Some programs actually
encourage wrong answers. There is a spelling program in which wrong
letters are pitched into a waste paper basket. This is much more exciting
than the tick which is the reward for the correct answer. The 'tutorial'
aspects of some programs and the rewards offered for correct responses
have been developed to a fine art, especially in some American software.
In such programs, both the teacher and student may appreciate the finesse
shown. Teachers concerned with language need always to ask whether
such approaches are in accord with a philosophy in which language is
regarded as a food for personal growth rather than a sequence of skills to
be tested.

A more versatile use of the computer in such a scenario allows the student to create his own quiz for the benefit of other students. The format
is taken care of by the computer; the information finding, checking and
typing belongs to the student. The results may not always be accurate, but

the educational gain to the question-setter is surely greater. Two programs which permit this are called MAKE A QUIZ and DO A QUIZ, and are included in the Microprimer pack provided for British primary schools.

Simulations

A simulation program displays information relating to a real or imaginary scenario. The program will respond to input in a way which is consistent with the situation, allowing the user to explore and understand it. If the simulation is to succeed, it must accurately represent (albeit in simplified form) the real phenomenon on which it is based: i.e., the model must be accurate.

Simulation programs have a special use in the area of language, where such programs have encouraged a whole new area of topic-based education. Most British primary schools adopt a topic-based approach to learning, where all the usual primary subjects are centred around a particular theme for a given period of time. For such an approach, topic webs have to be carefully thought out if nearly all subjects are to be covered adequately. In such a situation, the materials provided, and the ideas presented, by a program such as MARY ROSE (Ginn) can be invaluable and it would be hard indeed to misuse the material. It can, however, be done. A simulation program which does not fire the imagination of the teacher is not suitable for that teacher, and the children will gain little from merely 'doing' the program. In the end, personal preference is the surest way of judging a simulation.

On a simpler level, simulations in language work can be used to provide an interesting experience whilst encouraging the completion of a particular task, such as that of sentence ordering. If this is the case, the object of the program should be clear and not lost within the simulation.

In all forms of simulation program, the user interface is important. The program should not be so complex to drive that time is wasted and frustration caused. This is particularly true of programs for primary children. If the program is to be used on many occasions as a director of operations, it is helpful if it contains some method of identifying the user, such as a personal password, so that a child or group can return to the same place in a program that was left. WORDHOARD from the Cheshire Language Centre has just such a facility. The saving of an adventure game has long been a part of the features of a commercial game, and should be looked for in an educational package. Students should be able to pick up a game from the point where they left off, rather than recommence.

Databases

In Britain there is now a widespread concern with the development of 'information skills'. The now defunct Schools Council distributed to all secondary schools a booklet, *Information Skills in the Secondary Curriculum*, in

1981. It stressed the importance of helping children to find effective strategies for selecting, evaluating, recording and using information across the curriculum and at all ages. The development of appropriate reading strategies for study concerns the English teacher in British secondary schools at least as much as other teachers. With the spread of computerized information systems many are coming to use such systems themselves, often concentrating on the importance of interpreting and communicating information in its many forms.

The most obvious use of information retrieval in schools involves the use of 'databases', and in this form students will soon become acquainted with their all-pervading effect on their lives. Different databases are appropriate for different purposes, but it is worth learning from the common experience that buying databases can be like buying freezers: they never seem to be large or complex enough to deal with future needs. They also have a jargon of their own, which needs to be understood before reading any literature on the subject.

It is useful to know that there are 'relational' and 'hierarchical' databases, and to know the distinction. Relational databases are those of which one can ask questions. Such questions are framed using a limited selection of codewords and symbols, such as: QUERY TEXT SUB "HAMLET" AND CHARACTER NIDENT "HAMLET". In the particular system being used, this means: 'Show me any references to Hamlet made by any character other than Hamlet'. Hierarchical databases are based on a tree structure, and 'viewdata' systems such as Prestel in Britain are characterized by a series of indexes which allow the user to proceed from the more general to the more particular in search of a specific 'frame' of information (as well as allowing them to proceed directly to a specified frame). Progams such as MEP's EDFAX which allow teachers and students to generate such systems for themselves have been used to advantage by English teachers and primary teachers in Britain to allow children to create their own electronic 'magazines'.

Some teachers have also used relational databases as tools in classroom simulations, such as simulations of the problems of assigning priorities to applications for local council housing. Not only does their use in such scenarios reflect real applications, but it can lend focus to what can become highly-charged discussion of the moral and political issues.

Constructing a relational database involves a classificatory use of language. In order to judge whether they may suit your needs it is useful to be aware of the kinds of classification that such systems require, as well as the technical terms with which one needs to be familiar when comparing the capabilities of one system with another. Let us take a simple example. Suppose it is required to build a list of the names, addresses and dates of birth of the boys in form 1E. The *file* could be named 1EBoys. The information for each boy constitutes a *record*, and the database needs to be set up with *fields*, e.g. surname, forename, street, town, date of birth. It is therefore sensible, before choosing a database, to have some idea of the complexity of information that has to be handled. At a simple level, if 10 fields per record are required, a database allowing 8 is inadequate. Most databases only permit fields of a particular length; again the length should be checked against that which is required.

Once set up, a search can be made of the entered data according to the user's stated criteria. Using the same example as before, a search could be made for those boys whose name is Jones and whose date of birth is not 10 May 1975. More complex searches can be made; perhaps of those whose surname ends in . . . son, whose first name is not Alan, and whose birthday is in May. The complexity of the search that can be made is dependent on the program. A 'sort' can often be made; i.e., the information rearranged according to some criterion, and resaved. Again, it is essential to have some idea of the purpose before choosing a system.

Another factor should not be overlooked. Some database programs have pre-formed files available for purchase. Some containing census data or extensive literary texts would be very time-consuming to set up. When choosing a database package it is worth remembering that for such applications it may be an advantage if existing files can be obtained.

Children have a fascination for databases, and the collecting and ordering of data for inclusion in a database are valuable activities, not least in logic and co-operation. The whole process can serve as a valuable focus for purposeful group discussion. The entering and manipulation of the data should, however, be as simple as possible. FACTFILE, produced by Cambridge Microsoftware is a particularly good example of a starter database. The child is prompted throughout the entering and editing using a menu approach. For simplicity, the terms 'record' and 'field' are replaced by 'items', which can be identified individually, and 'headings'. The searches cannot be complex but are probably sufficient at this level. Some more powerful databases use the same menu-driven approach and there is no doubt that these are the quickest with which to become familiar. Others use a command mode and for students and teachers unfamiliar with this method of control they can be difficult, if not impossible to use for the first few times. A database package is not the best way of learning to use command-structured programs; the advantage of such a mode, once mastered, is enormous versatility and plenty of help to hand. Inevitably, complex sorts and searches require using documentation, as queries must usually be entered in particular forms, and it is here that a person selecting a database should cast a critical eye. If the documentation is confusing, hours of frustration, not to mention lost and corrupt data, are inevitable.

Databases cannot be assessed quickly and the experience of others is the most helpful guide.[1]

Word Processing
The first evaluation of a word-processing package should be a personal evaluation of what is required on a teaching level. The second should be an assessment of the system as a competent accepter, displayer and manipulator of text.

There are programs which teach about word-processing, but these are better classed as simulations. There are expensive business word-processors which provide all office facilities. In between these extremes, there are many smaller systems designed for schools and small businesses. The packages available for schools are sometimes contained in a 'chip' which has to be fitted into the computer, so such a system cannot be bought and used immediately as can a typewriter. The job of fitting the chip is not difficult but is sensibly left to a competent person. A word-processing package is of little use without a printer. Decisions must therefore be made about the type of printer, as this can seriously effect some of the facilities offered by the system.

Another area which requires attention is the documentation of the package. If it is to be used to teach word-processing to children then that documentation must be directed at a level which is understandable by children. Some packages require a high degree of familiarity with computer processes if their documentation is to be understood.

For teaching word-processing, it is also reasonable to hope for adequate help for students within the program. Many do not give this; EDWORD, published by Clwyd Technics Ltd., does. When a 'beep' is heard, a mistake in the use of the program has occurred, and the error can be ascertained by pressing a predetermined key. In this package also, the student is kept informed by notices as to which facilities (e.g. formatting or inserting) are currently in use, and the text to be dealt with is highlighted. The choice of page length, margin size, etc., are also chosen from a spreadsheet.

If the package is to be used solely in school administration, a different set of criteria is needed. A document could be longer than the computer is able to hold in memory. Editing into and out of memory is therefore a desirable feature. A facility for retyping the same letter with variable inserts could also be valuable.

If the word-processing package is to be used not to train children in the use of word-processors for office work but rather to encourage children to produce good prose without the excessive burden of correcting and copying, another set of factors becomes important. The size of type on the screen and the ease of editing are two such considerations. An early example of a system designed to meet children's needs as writers rather than to teach them how to use an office word-processor was the American BANK STREET WRITER. Now there is also the MILLIKEN WORD PRO-

CESSOR for the Apple.[2]

There are a number of books which may serve as a useful introduction to writing with the computer. *Word Processing for Beginners* by Susan Curran (Granada) is good. Some books on the topic are written in a questionnaire form for easy use in assessing software. Personal recommendation is also most important, although someone who is familiar with a program may have become used to its shortcomings and may forget to mention them in the course of discussing it. Look at various packages. A computer shop is probably the best place to examine software. Go away and list what is needed, then return and re-assess the system.

Computers can also be used for the remote exchange of information. This can be via the telephone network. At this point, the horizons broaden. Instant communication between schools in different parts of the country and the ability to interrogate national databanks are both facilities which will soon become available. There is no reason, however, to ignore the possibilities of internal communication within the school. It is a principle which is used even in the self-contained QUILL package produced by Bolt Beranek and Newman in the US, allowing children to put their writing into the system to be shared with other users.

A clear understanding of types of programs gives the potential user a better idea of the programs which could be used with confidence and success.

Educational content

The final stage of evaluation requires an assessment of educational content. This aspect should be foremost in the teacher's mind throughout the preliminary checking. It has to be assumed that the idea behind a program is appealing, or it would not have reached the stage of being considered for purchase.

The accuracy of information in a computer program should not need to be questioned, but it has to be. On a simple level, spellings are often inaccurate. Even more seriously, some programs on the market until quite recently, gave wrong information. In such a case, complaints must be made, and the program, if already purchased, sent back.

The program does not have to be tailored to the curriculum, but it is essential that it is relevant and that the teaching process would be improved by the use of a computer. The time required to use the software adequately is also important. Some commercial packages make a considerable meal out of a minor part of a syllabus, which could more easily be taught by conventional methods or a shorter computer program.

Further questions should come to mind. Does the program use language suited to the intended age-range of the users? Is the program consistent in its language throughout? Are there adequate worksheets and follow-up materials, or does the program provide the whole learning experience? All these should be considered.

Every teacher has a different teaching style and a program should complement this, not conflict with it.

The true measure of any instructional program is whether it teaches what it is intended to teach. Trying it out on students and recording their reactions are sensible precautions but not always possible; however, a teacher ought to be a good judge. The final question is: 'Does the program provide a valid educational experience?'.

The following is a description of one program for which the answer to the previous question would be an emphatic 'Yes'.

MALLORY MANOR

The program MALLORY MANOR is written by Anita Straker and simulates a *Cluedo* game. A burglary takes place and the user, as detective, has to recover the stolen objects and find the thief. The manor has 25 rooms and 12 occupants. As the rooms and occupants are arranged randomly, interesting, not to say exciting, combinations of people and places can occur. A new game is provided every time.

The program is presented well, with large text; it is robust and provides an unusual challenge. As an educational experience, it offers opportunities for practising note-taking and the selection and ordering of information. It is an exercise in logical thinking and deduction. It could, however, be used as the springboard for a large number of different projects. A dramatic production, an investigation into the social life of a country house with servants and masters at the turn of the century, and an investigation into the role of the police in society are all aspects that could be developed. Further areas of interest which suggest themselves are forensic science, the value society places on possessions, the modelling of the manor and mineralogy.

Programs such as MALLORY MANOR, which led themselves to a wide variety of lesson plans, suggest the richness of well-designed educational software. Such software does not limit teachers' creativity nor constrain students' involvement. When evaluating and selecting software, teachers should be alert to a program's potential for wider application, bringing to bear a broader vision than perhaps even that of the program's designers. This will immeasurably enhance the teacher's own 'computer literacy', resulting quite naturally in greater benefits to the students.[3]

6 Designing Software

DANIEL CHANDLER

Many Language Arts teachers who become interested in the potential of the computer as a learning tool are quick to ask: 'Why aren't programs being designed to meet our needs?'. The easy answer is, of course, that they are beginning to be. In Britain, for instance, the new software house called CLASS (Cambridge Language Arts Software Services) is specifically concerned with providing for this demand. However, programs which meet the needs of teachers concerned with particular curricular objectives are indeed few and far between. The main reason for this is that computer courseware of any worth is expensive to produce: less narrowly curricular educational software has a larger market.

I am hardly a usual advocate of the usefulness of market forces in education. In this case, however, I consider it to be a fortunate consideration. Certainly I regard the computer as a potentially powerful learning tool, but I must candidly admit that I do not believe that we should be attempting to produce computer programs which are narrowly specific to 'subjects' in institutional education. And as a former English teacher in British secondary schools my feeling is that producing computer programs specifically to serve curricular objectives for English teaching is a sad phenomenon indeed; I had always regarded the English classroom as one of the few areas in schools in which children might have at least some opportunities for autonomous exploration of their own thoughts and feelings. Of course, especially in North America, the computer is being widely used as a tool to support the smooth-running of the curriculum, but as I wrote recently, where this priority dictates the use of computers in schools the kinds of applications involved tend to trivialize the potential of both the computer and the child.[1] Untrammelled by instructional software, the computer is, quite simply, too interesting to fit neatly into the rigidly compartmentalized curricula that characterize British and North American secondary education. For me, it is yet another justifiable challenge to such curricula, and could more hopefully be regarded as a subversive device in the hands of enlightened educators.

Many adults who have their own microcomputers at home use them as powerful tools in such applications as word-processing, and data storage and retrieval. If adults find these tools useful, why do such applications take second place to 'educational' software in so many schools? Teachers sometimes respond to this by saying that most of the popular general-purpose tools were not designed with young users in mind. This is true, of course, and it is worth asking why programs such as word-processing packages couldn't be designed more simply in the first place: it is not only children who can find them awkward to manipulate. The general quality of software design will probably improve in time but it is doubtful whether commercial producers will ever be particularly concerned with the needs of young users. Therefore, in the short-term at least, it does seem appropriate that 'educational software' projects should concentrate on producing general-purpose tools which put children's needs first.

It is difficult to disagree with Seymour Papert's general principle that 'what is good for professionals is good for children'.[2] However, the problem with many existing software development projects for children is that the computer systems and budgets open to them hardly reflect those available to the producers of software for 'professional' applications: consequently, the tendency is that tools which are offered for children are often far less potent than those aimed at the professional market. National and local expenditure on computers in education would seem to be far better used for supporting the provision of systems at least as flexible as those found in the homes of serious enthusiasts and in the production of limited 'toolkits' of software, rather than for providing minimal systems (without printers, or even in many British schools, without disc-drives) and trying to produce software for computerizing the curriculum.

Thus far I have not made clear what role, if any, Language Arts teachers may have in developing software. In Britain at least this has been an area which has been given low priority, and yet, as Brent Robinson demonstrates elsewhere in this book, whatever the application, the computer is a medium for reading and writing (albeit one with many unfamiliar characteristics). Anyone involved in the design of software tools ought to be conscious of the needs of readers and writers (of whatever age): the fact is that this consciousness is rare indeed. Teachers concerned with reading, writing, talking and listening could have a very valuable role in contributing to the design of more general-purpose computer-based tools which they themselves could use with children. Indeed I have often advocated the urgent need for far more teachers of the language arts to become involved in software design rather than allowing the production of 'educational' software to be dominated by programmers and mathematicians.

Not every teacher needs to learn programming (although none should be deterred by the thought that programming is not a 'creative' activity), but teachers who intend to use computers should also be aware that they can make important contributions to the design of software if they are prepared to make the effort to become familiar with the medium. Professional programmers can't be assumed to understand or be aware of the changes in educational philosophy which may have made the creative role of 'English' in education quite foreign to their own experience. Imaginative and progressive English teachers who possess a high level of professional programming expertise are rare indeed: time is not likely to dramatically increase their numbers. The most effective strategy for the production of software in which the priorities of the Language Arts are accorded central importance is a collaborative effort involving both professional programmers and educationalists with a deep commitment to the language arts.

What can be done?

Any teacher who is to play a role in software design needs first to have some familiarity with what microcomputers can do. This can only be achieved by using them, but this use need not be restricted to explicitly 'educational' applications. A general awareness of what mainframe computers are used to do in society at large is not adequate: anyone who wants to know what microcomputers can do should acquire a comfortable familiarity with some general-purpose tools such as word-processors and databases; well-designed games and simulations will also help to expand their awareness of features of the medium. Where local education authorities do not provide teachers with opportunities to explore such applications they may find it useful to play with computers in the informal atmosphere of a local 'user group' (i.e. a group of local enthusiasts who use a particular kind of microcomputer) or in a computer club.

Even where they do not intend to become involved in software design, English teachers interested in using computers need to ask themselves whether they have reached a stage where they have a working understanding of the microcomputer as a new medium.

• *Firstly, have you come to realize that the computer is a medium just as capable of manipulating words as it is of 'number crunching'?*

The computer is a general-purpose device for manipulating any kind of symbol, and it consequently has applications in processing text, synthesizing sounds and generating graphics just as it does in manipulating numerical and other data. The educational potential of text manipulation has tended to be neglected, which is perhaps hardly surprising given the background of most of those usually entrusted with responsibility for the use of the computer as a resource in schools. This in itself is one reason why English teachers should become more involved in so-called 'computer literacy' initiatives.

The computer's capability of manipulating words should not, however, be misinterpreted as the capability to comprehend meaning: despite many superficial examples which may lure us into believing otherwise, artificial intelligence research has not resulted (as yet at least) in microcomputers which can genuinely understand the user's natural language. Some 'educational' software employs some imitation of understanding on the part of the program, usually in tutorial applications. Such applications may allow the user to type in full sentence responses to computer-initiated questions, and rely on matching expected and actual responses. Currently at least, microcomputer-based educational software which attempts to do this is doomed to result in many failures; more importantly, it may also frustrate a real understanding of the limitations of computers.

The manipulation of words can, however, involve far more than the generation of 'personalized circulars', which might be the only concept which would spring to mind with an English teacher who had only the vaguest experience of computers and a healthy cynicism about the use of computers in business applications.

● *Secondly, can you see ways in which the use of the computer for a particular purpose might be preferable to trying to use the more conventional technology of ink and paper?*

Those who have not seen for themselves alternatives to a model absorbed from the conventions of the printed book will not be able to make very effective contributions in a team designing software for serious educational applications. There is a glut of mindless 'educational' software in which the computer is no more than an expensive page-turner or electronic slot-and-filler 'workbook'. The microcomputer is a poor substitute for a printed book, but as a medium it has properties which may sometimes make it far more flexible and appropriate. Such features include 'branching', interaction, management and 'learning'.

Some properties of the medium

Branching is based on a tree-like structure commonly employed in program design. For instance, a computerized database may involve starting from a general index, choosing an option, and then 'branching' to a succession of increasingly specific subsidiary indexes until one reaches the particular 'frame' required. Such a structure allows users to leap around from one 'menu' of options to another in some programs, a far less sequential process than is usually favoured by the 'frozen' medium of print.

'Interactive' is a term all too often used to refer to instructional programs which fire questions at the user, allow them the option of responding 'yes' or 'no', and then pronounce the responses clinically 'correct' or 'incorrect'. But a more imaginative use of the medium may involve an interaction in which the user is able to manipulate the computer for his or her own purposes like a tool. Where such a use of the computer does not involve linguistic interaction the program might more usefully be described as 'responsive': a quality which is certainly not found in conventional books.

The role of the computer as manager is obvious in computer-based games. The program can incorporate the rules of a game, so that the computer can act both as framework and umpire, leaving the players free to concentrate on strategies. This is just as advantageous in other educational tools, such as in simulations. This management role may allow the program to control the pacing of the activities, so that, for instance, in a newsdesk simulation, news items could be realistically fed into the office at moments which even the teacher could not predict. Indeed, perhaps the greatest advantage of using the computer as manager in such circumstances is that it takes the role of captain and referee away from the teacher, allowing her to withdraw, to be an observer or to participate on equal terms with the children. No print-based resource will double as an organizer like this.

Another un-booklike feature of a few computer programs is an in-built ability for the program to 'learn' from the user. The simplest and best-known example of this is in the popular ANIMAL game referred to elsewhere (see Appendix 2). So far, other examples in educational computing are rare, but there would seem to be a great deal of scope for programs which allow the user to 'teach' the computer about language, so that, for instance, it might become an increasingly formidable partner in a word-based version of the logic game, MASTERMIND.

Knowing the limitations of your system

An American designer of software for the Language Arts, Dr Irene Thomas, has commented that 'Any teacher who is trained to work with text rather than with numbers, yet who has fantasies about designing software, would be startled to an abrupt halt when faced with . . . memory and screen specifications. And perhaps that is as it should be. It's time that teachers understood the enormous demands put upon a designer and the time it takes to produce even the simplest program'.[3]

Anyone who is to take a major part in the design of software must know enough about programming and the particular computer to be used in order to be able to produce adequate technical specifications. Although any classroom teacher can play some part in the development of software (and indeed many British software development projects are characterized by the involvement of classroom teachers), the role of 'program designer' is one which the average classroom teacher is not likely to have the time and specialist knowledge to adopt. The most effective approach to the development of powerful educational tools in both Britain and the US has involved design teams. The composition of such teams varies, but a typical team might include one or two teachers with some powerful ideas, a specialist software designer, a professional programmer, and disinterested advisers to help with editing and (hopefully) publishing. The more technical information which we will now present is therefore provided simply as an introduction to some of the factors involved in the formal design process rather than a do-it-yourself guide for individual teachers hoping to design and develop programs alone.

Size of memory
Before embarking on program design, it is essential to be aware of the limitations of the computer system you plan to use. The most obvious is its immediate memory capacity, measured in 'K'. There's no point in planning the development of a computerized Encyclopaedia Galactica if all you've got is a cassette-based microcomputer with only 8 K of usable memory. For any serious applications you must have a disc-based system with a minimum of 32 K; most applications would greatly benefit from larger systems. Exploring this topic would quickly become very technical, but we will confine ourselves here to information useful to potential program designers with a special interest in text-handling. While the examples used below refer to hardware common in the UK (and not in the US), the design issues are general.

Briefly, 1 K is about 1000 'bytes', or memory-boxes. In terms of text, these could contain about 1000 individual alphabetical letters, so that a program which left around 1 K free for text might have room for about 150 words at any one time (although larger quantities could be handled by loading and storing short chunks when needed). Memory capacities for BBC systems are given in Table 1.

Table 1: Available memory on BBC microcomputer systems (K).

MODE	0	1	2	3	4	5	6	7
Disc	5.9	5.9	5.9	9.9	15.9	15.9	17.9	24.9
Cassette	8.7	8.7	8.7	12.7	18.7	18.7	20.7	27.7

Even if you know how much immediate memory space is available on the system you plan to use, this could be misleading, since if you have a disc system, a program could be designed to use discs for storing 'files' of data (such as text), and a disc might have a 100 K storage capacity.

Whatever the initially available memory, only a proportion of it will be available for such things as a user's text: the program itself obviously takes up some of the space, and only when the programmer has some idea of the complexity of your program idea will it be possible to estimate the amount of space likely to be left for other purposes such as storing children's texts. Only then may this kind of table prove useful to those more used to writing on paper: Table 2.

Table 2: Memory consumed by words

Available memory	No. of words	Equiv. pages	Available memory	No. of words	Equiv. pages
4 K	682	1.5	24 K	4096	9.1
8 K	1365	3.0	32 K	5461	12.1
12 K	2048	4.5	48 K	8192	18.2
16 K	2730	6.1	64 K	10922	24.3

Note: Based on average word-length of 6 letters, average page of 450 words

Graphics options

Text is not the only rapid consumer of memory. If you intend to use graphics (illustrations) then programmers need to know the smallest number of colours which would be needed, and how detailed your drawings would have to be in order to decide, for instance, with the BBC computer, what graphics mode to choose. The finer the line required, the more memory the graphics will consume.

Screen dimensions for text

To design the 'frames' of text which will appear on the screen you will need also to know the dimensions of the screen in terms of letters per line and lines per frame, Figure 1.

It may seem particularly important to have up to 80 letters per line (perhaps when using the computer for substantial amounts of writing). Or you might want the program to use very large letters for display to a group, although legibility might lead one to prefer 'teletext'-style lettering rather

←   characters per line   →

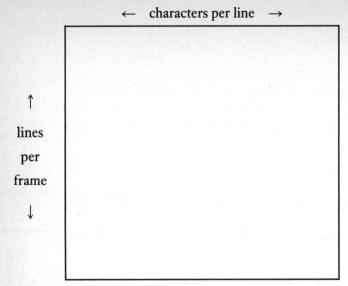

Figure 1   Defining screen dimensions for text

than the flattened lettering familiar from video-games. If a particular number of letters per line is a priority, one needs to remember that this may also constrain other options. Frame dimensions for BBC systems are given in Table 3.

Table 3: Frame dimensions for text on BBC micro systems.

MODE:	0	1	2	3	4	5	6	7a*	7b*
chars/line	80	40	20	80	40	20	40	40	39
lines	32	32	32	25	32	32	25	25	12

* 7a=normal MODE 7; 7b='teletext' double-height characters.

Designers need to bear in mind that on some TV sets the top or bottom line of the display may not be visible. Some programmers consequently avoid using these two lines. Also, even with a system which can cope with 80 characters per line, these may only be readable on a good quality video monitor.

Disc-drives and printers

Apart from the kind of computer being used, the programmer will also need to know whether you will want the program to be designed for use with a disc-drive, for use with a cassette-recorder, or for use with both.

The design options open for disc-only programs are far greater than those open for cassette-only programs, and a program designed for use with both cassette and disc may not be as flexible and powerful as one designed for use only with disc. The lucky few may also have the option of using dual disc-drives, which offer an even greater range of design options. (Such a system would, for instance, be ideal for software which involved storing large quantities of text on one disc and having spelling checked against substantial wordbanks stored on another.)

After determining what disc facilities are available, you need to decide whether you will have access to a computer printer. In many schools the printer may be a central resource: texts can be stored on disc and taken to this central location for printing. Given the importance of print on paper to the concerns of English teachers, a departmental or classroom printer would obviously be far more convenient.

What kind of program?

So far, the decision-making listed has been purely reactive: what constraints does your system oblige you to conform to? After this necessary stage, the designer's most important role is that of an inventor, a visionary, a poet who can creatively explore the new medium. This is where so many narrowly technical programmers have fallen down, and it is where the creative imaginations of such people as English teachers are most desperately needed. With this perspective one may usefully reflect on the limitations of your particular system in a way which makes a virtue of necessity: just as the restrictions of the sonnet form can be regarded as a spur to creative exploitation, so the technical constraints within which you must operate can be viewed positively as a way of forcing you to focus on your problem with a freshness of vision.

When novices approach this stage, cynics are wont to remark that this is an example of the computer as a solution in search of a problem. Inevitably, until the designer is thoroughly familiar with the medium, exploring its possibilities will continue to be an important aspect of the process. However, the most obvious answer to the cynics is probably that imaginative English teachers are hardly short of problems for which they are always ready to seek alternative strategies! The best starting point for program design may be the consideration of problem areas.

Individual English teachers will obviously differ in what they consider these problems to be; an old list of my own includes (in no particular order):

- making small group discussion more effective
- inspiring children to want to write

- trying to develop the drafting habit
- encouraging extensive reading
- developing strategies for effective intensive reading
- making all such activities an integral part of a 'language workshop' approach rather than trying to teach isolated 'skills'
- trying to ensure that all children would be able to play a part in these activities regardless of 'ability'.

This list was conceived without any consideration of computers, but it did not take long, in the light of these priorities, to perceive the kinds of activity in which the microcomputer might be of use to me as an English teacher at a progressive community comprehensive school. Suitable applications which sprang to mind included word-processing and data-handling, which involved using the computer as a general-purpose tool, and also simulations and simulation-games, in which the computer acts as a generator and focus for purposeful group discussion and 'playful thinking'. My list of priorities also made it easy for me to see ways in which I would certainly not want to use a microcomputer.

I was looking for 'real' uses of microcomputers – ways in which both adults and children outside institutional education might choose to use microcomputers for their own purposes. People in the 'real world' do not use computers for 'skill and drill' exercises: why should school students (some of whom are able to write their own computer programs outside school) put up with the computer as a mechanical instructor simply because they are in school?

The starting point is to decide what one's broad educational priorities are, and in what kind of area the support of a powerful tool might prove productive. One can then move on to considering what kind of tools might have a particular appeal for children. Next one needs to decide how far to incorporate the context in the software (are you aiming at creating a general-purpose tool such as a word-processor, or would it be more effective to create a 'front-page' package for a newspaper simulation, which might incorporate word-processing facilities?).

Whereas the creation of software for programmed learning is a relatively straightforward (if longwinded) activity involving a great deal of convergent thinking, open-ended software demands creative designers who are bold enough not to be blinkered by what they have already seen done elsewhere. There is no formula for generating specific ideas for such software; my only suggestion here is that brainstorming with several of one's colleagues can be both stimulating and productive, but that, in my experience, once you have chosen a likely possibility the refining of the idea is best left to one or two enthusiasts who have at least some experience of the practical difficulties of programming.

What sort of design?

Once a program idea has been fixed upon, the next stage involves devising a suitable design concept. This always involves the balancing of two critical priorities: flexibility and ease of use.

Programs which are designed to be simple for beginners to use may take the user gradually through each step involved in the activity: in doing so they may take not only the sequencing but also many other decisions away from the user. And the whole process may become unnecessarily slow. Text-hungry 'help' options may reduce the space available to make the program do anything useful. Such programs also discriminate in favour of a very specific (and not very creative) personal learning style. On the other hand, a powerful but skeletal program with many options open at all times (and perhaps with the secrets of successful operation involving careful reading of the printed documentation) may leave a beginner drowning rather than increasing her autonomy as a learner.

One might argue that a solution would be to produce two separate versions of the same program idea: one designed to introduce the beginner to the system, and the other designed to offer more experienced users a far wider range of options. However, this is an expensive option, and one might counter it by suggesting that what the beginner may need is simply a gentle and supportive introduction to the flexible system from someone experienced in its use.

There is a parallel to this issue in the broader context of the 'locus of control' when learners use computers. I have argued against drill and practice, which resides at one end of the locus of control, in which the control of the activity lies with the computer program, and in favour of the use of content-free tools, in which the locus of control is far closer to the user. In choosing a design concept for a tool-like program one's options range from prompting the user at each stage (a 'prompt-driven' design), through 'menu-driven' designs (in which the user is offered a series of options at key points in the program), to options controlled by 'function keys' or 'command languages' which offer all the program's options simultaneously (see Chapter 5 by Diana Thomson). Selecting an appropriate framework is, as I have indicated, a question of balancing the priorities of flexibility and ease of use, bearing in mind the particular needs of the intended users.

Developing specifications

Professional programming is expensive, and it is to no one's advantage to leave programming specifications imprecise. Having an idea and a design concept is not enough: to give you what you want the programmer must know precisely what you want the user to see and be able to do throughout the program. With the design concept chosen, the next step in developing the specifications is to draw up 'screen charts' for the program, showing exactly what the user would see on the screen at each point (if the design concept is linear or branching), or more abstractly what would happen under every circumstance (if the program is driven by function keys or a command language); for example, what pressing a 'swap' function key might allow the user to do to her text.

Obviously, designing a linear or branching program is easier for the beginner than designing a more abstract system, because one can regard the screen as a sort of storyboard. A very effective strategy in developing such a design is to regard the whole problem as being like a jigsaw. Areas of your program idea may be fairly clear-cut to you; others may at first seem a little hazy. Start by thinking about a small chunk of your program. What might the user see on the screen? What options would be open to the user at this point, and what effect would they have on what she would see next? Try cutting up sheets of paper into rectangles about half the size of small index cards, and treat them like 'frames' in the program on which you can depict what would be seen on the screen at any one point. Try to form a sequence of some kind by setting them out on an A3 sheet of paper (you may need several such sheets glued together into a much larger rectangular sheet). Where the sequence is broken (because the user has options) start to develop a tree-like (or root-like) pattern of frames, pencilling arrows between those which follow.

Talking to programmers

When you have finally drawn up screen-charts which you have explained and agreed with your colleagues, you will now need to discuss the idea in detail with a programmer. The immediate problem of course is where to find one. For teachers in Britain the first step would certainly be to seek out the county adviser for computer education (if there is one) to ascertain whether any support might be forthcoming from that direction. Some counties have educational computing centres with staff who may be able to assist.

You can also find out what expertise is available within your own institution – both amongst teachers and students. However, you need to be fairly sure that whoever takes on your project is both capable of handling it and willing to accept the lengthy process of revision which is almost invariably involved. You may hear people saying that they can write a program over a weekend, but such people are usually writing fairly clear-cut programs for themselves. It has already been indicated that tool-like programs are far more complex to create than explicitly instructional software, but you also need to bear in mind that however fully you thought you had specified your program, and however clearly you thought you had explained it to other colleagues who intend to use it, you might not have fully realized how a literal implementation of your idea might turn out. If you do not feel reasonably comfortable about asking the programmer to tackle fairly substantial revisions in the light of the prototype you may find yourself using the program more out of courtesy than any educational justification. This caveat will obviously apply whether you are considering a teacher or student in your own school or another school, a parent or a hobbyist from a local computer club. A professional is therefore obviously preferable, and a programmer employed by a local education authority should be used to working with teachers who may not necessarily be very familiar with the microcomputer.

Don't expect to be able to develop a tool-based program in under six months with a part-time programmer: major projects may take a year or more. Even if the first version is created within two to three months, a series of revisions you may decide upon in the light of the prototype is likely to extend the development time to at least six months, after which trials of the materials may turn up obscure bugs or lead to further modifications, and not only 'Users' Notes' but other support materials may well be an integral part of the whole package which could take several months to prepare. If such an expensive job is worth doing, it's certainly worth doing well, and to be worth the effort, the materials clearly need to be likely to be used as far more than a one-off option.

It is an advantage to consult a programmer before going to the trouble of drawing up specifications, since what you propose may not be technically possible with the system you have available. However, some of the best software is that which was once declared 'impossible' by a programmer, so, if you have the luxury of a choice of programmers you may be wise to seek a second opinion. You may well have to accept compromises, but if these threaten to compromise the very value of the idea itself, back out: technology should serve you, not the other way about.

Checklist of stages for the design team

- Ensure that everyone has some familiarity with what microcomputers can do.
- Check which microcomputer system is available to you: make, memory-size, screen dimensions for text, and whether you will be able to use discs and a printer.
- Brainstorm to focus on a problem area and then on a way in which the computer might help.
- With the support of your local authority English and Computing Advisers try to find out whether a software package which might meet this need already exists: if it does, is it adequate for your needs?

- Fix on an appropriate design concept.
- Draw up screen charts (bearing in mind screen dimensions for text).
- Write program design specifications.
- Ask the programmer to develop a realization of the idea.
- Agree on any modifications (note that this stage will usually cycle with the previous one for some time).
- Return to the programmer for error-trapping, debugging and testing.
- Develop any print materials which may usefully form part of the whole package (including notes for users).
- Try out the materials with pilot groups, seeking their reactions and suggestions.
- Implement any improvements where feasible. (Keen students may be helpful here if you've lost the goodwill of the programmer by now!)
- Decide where to draw the line in regarding the package as 'finished' (over-refining is a common problem).
- Share the package with colleagues in other schools. (Don't neglect any possibilities this may offer for liaison with primary schools or with parents.)

Much of this chapter has been devoted to presenting background information and points of reference for those interested in becoming involved in the process of designing computer software for the Language Arts. But more critical than an awareness of such details is the concept of the design team, in which educators and computer specialists work together. Whether such a method of working is open to all teachers with powerful ideas for software tools is largely a question of local politics. Full-time teachers need to be given time to take part in program design teams; they need access to professional programmers and designers. Design teams for developing educational software are quite impossible without the full support of local education authorities or government agencies such as the MEP in Britain.

Another key issue is that there is still an acute shortage of specialist program designers with an imaginative flair, an educational background (especially in the Language Arts) and programming experience. Dr Thomas has suggested that: 'We . . . ought to be calling for the creation and support of a new class of computer professional – educational designers – to liaise with teachers and train programmers. These people might come from the ranks of former teachers or computer specialists/ advisers, or part-time teachers whose design-work time is ultimately paid for either by grants or by publishing companies'.[4] Whilst the role of a commercial sponsor might give rise to some concern in the context of the British educational system, the general principle seems to me to be just as applicable in the UK as in the US, and, once again, it would require official backing to stand any chance of success.

To quote from Dr Thomas's American perspective once more: 'Until teachers gain full appreciation for the process and defend their role in the process, they will have no role in the process; they will be totally at the mercy of the commercial hawkers and hacks . . . [and] commercial interests will have taken over the curriculum the way the textbook publishers have'.[5] In the UK, where textbook publishers do not wield such power in schools, teachers may be inclined to dismiss such fears. If they do, they may need to be reminded of the dangerous power of an impoverished curriculum which commercial concerns are already dictating for the vast British market for computer software in the home.[6]

7 The Dangers of Computers in Literacy Education: Who's in Charge Here?

DAVID DILLON

The use of computers is spreading widely through Western society and may profoundly change our lives. Computers are spreading into schools, too, and they have quickly become one of the most pressing concerns educators have had to deal with in some time. It appears they will remain an issue for some time to come.

While computer applications in schools range through the whole curriculum, their impact has been greatest in maths and in the area of our concern, literacy. Like all significant issues, the computer has two vocal and strong sides, one claiming educational salvation through computers, the other claiming in that way lies damnation. Clearly, computers are a two-edged sword that promise benefits and dangers. Indeed, the benefits and dangers are often at opposite ends of one basic dimension. This chapter will survey dangers in the use of computers in regard to literacy. Yet, by so doing, the potential benefits and strengths of computers should also be illuminated. I agree with Seymour Papert, author of *Mindstorms: Children, Computers, and Powerful Ideas*, that the major dimension or issue in their school use is one of control. Who is in charge of learning: machine or machine user? The way in which we resolve the issue will lead to either liberation or domestication for pupils.

The issue of control

The subtitle of this chapter, 'Who's in Charge Here?' is the title of a Canadian TV documentary on unemployment, broadcast in the fall of 1983. Thirty unemployed Canadians were invited and paid to participate in a four-day seminar in retreat-fashion ostensibly to discuss the unemployment situation and to generate possible solutions to the problems which could then be proposed to government and business. After describing what it was like to be unemployed, most participants concluded their remarks with a statement that something needed to be done about unemployment. Although a small team of psychologists were supposedly in charge of the seminar, it became readily apparent that they were not playing traditional leadership roles. They responded to participants' comments, questions, and suggestions with bland, non-committal remarks, further questions, blank stares, or even departure from the room. Regardless of the response of the 'leader', participants did not offer possible solutions, but usually lapsed quickly into silence, waiting and hoping for someone else to speak. The frustration and anger built up and by the third day some participants were reduced to tears. One of the more vocal speakers threatened for two days to leave but when finally he did on the morning of the fourth day, he returned after only a brief absence. A few did leave without any announcement. Several shouted threateningly at the 'leaders'. One man lashed out in angry frustration by knocking over furniture at the end of one session. The refrain continued, 'Someone should do something!'.

Then, toward the end of the seminar, the light dawned on the group. They saw exactly what the leaders had planned and had wanted participants to see, indeed to experience. Microcosmically, in that small-scale, four-day retreat, participants were experiencing what they had been living macrocosmically in Canadian society, namely a lack of any sense of control over what was happening to them and an apparent lack of response to their needs by those who were supposed to be in control, their leaders. The seminar participants railed not so much against anyone else's oppression and control over them, for there was very little, if any, there. Rather they cursed the absence of someone else's responsibility for them and unknowingly their own impotence in the face of a power vacuum. Normally their lives are controlled in many ways and they are – perhaps uncritically – used to it. When that control is removed, they simply do not know how to seize control for themselves. No one took responsibility and thus they all sank deeper in the mire.

This realization brought tears of relief to some and stunned silence to others as they began to realize whose responsibility they were – their own. Some of the participants appeared to feel even worse as a result of their fear of this responsibility and a stubborn, uncomprehending frustration of how they could possibly do something themselves about their own unemployment. The group, of course, never completed their original task of proposing solutions for others to implement, but many participants left the retreat with new awareness. I don't know what happened to any of them afterwards. I was left wondering if these people's lack of a sense of control over their lives was a cause, rather than a result, of their unemployment. For instance, their situation stood in stark contrast to that of the producer of the documentary, Alan King, who had assertively used high unemployment as a means of creating work for himself.

A long – and tangential – introduction? In one way, yes. In another, the story contains the basic message of this chapter. Let me turn the perspective or lens I've used to look at this noncomputer situation on to some similar situations involving computers.

Judith Newman (1984a), a teacher educator, relates an experience she had while waiting in an outer office for an appointment. The secretary working there was using a microcomputer and was having difficulty making the procedure she was trying to run work for her. The directions for the use of the program were either incomplete or unclear and the secretary was stumped. Newman became involved in the problem out of interest. Although she had no experience with the specific machine the secretary was using, she had some sense of what operations microcomputers are capable of and the procedures for assessing them. She suggested the secretary bring the main menu to the screen to see what options were available and, when the necessary information wasn't there, to bring up some sub-menus that sounded promising. She finally found the procedure she wanted and Newman proposed specific input in response to prompt questions. The task was eventually accomplished. Newman reflected afterwards on how different her approach to the problem was from the secretary's. She had some experience with microcomputers and had an underlying pattern of understanding. What is more, she viewed the machine as a tool to help her accomplish her purposes. On the other hand, the secretary had no such notion, even if she understood the program technologically. It was a basic question of who was in charge, machine or machine user.

Newman (1984c) describes another comparable situation, analysing how different learners go about learning to use a word-processor:

> Robbie, age nine, was most interested in trying to write a story. He'd had fun playing computer games but he knew the computer could be used for writing, too. He asked me if he could write something and if I would help him.
>
> At home, Robbie has an Atari videogame computer. He was sitting in front of an Apple, an unfamiliar machine. 'How do you turn it on? he asked. I showed him the ON/OFF switch in back and let him turn it on. 'Now,' I said, 'the machine needs some instructions to tell it how to be used for writing.' We were about to use one of the word-processors I have been using. I showed him how to place the disc in the drive and load the program. Then I let him do it himself. When the prompt appeared on the screen I showed him how to enter edit mode and he was ready to begin.
>
> 'How do you underline?' Robbie asked as he settled himself at the keyboard. I explained that to him and he began typing. 'How do you get

capitals?' he asked, noticing the lower-case characters on the screen. I showed him. Next, he asked about correcting typing errors. I showed him three things: how to erase, how to move the cursor across text without erasing, and how to insert characters. I wrote all of these instructions on a notepad which I keep beside the computer so he could refer to them as he needed. That was sufficient information for him to be able to write for several minutes. However, as the screen filled, he wanted to return to the beginning of his text and asked for help. I showed him how to move his cursor to the top and the bottom of his text. I wrote these commands on the notepad as well, then left him on his own. About thirty minutes later he came to tell me he was finished and wanted help printing his story. At that point I wrote the instructions for exiting edit mode and returning to the prompt. Next I asked him what he wanted to call his story and explained how to save it on the disc. Then I wrote the instructions and printing his story and let him do it.

In all, Robbie worked for three-quarters of an hour and in that brief time was well on his way to becoming a user of microcomputer technology for writing.

Compare Robbie's experience with what one of Newman's teacher-students reported about her first word-processing experiences while responding to Newman's account of Robbie's experiences:

Probably one of the main reasons for my frustration was my attitude to using the computer. I felt that I had to sit down at the keyboard and figure out how everything worked before I felt comfortable using the computer as a vehicle for my writing. As it happened, time constraints forced me to push ahead, with text editing and learn things about the computer as I went along just like Robbie. So as I see it, my learning was no different than his, but my expectations about how I should learn were; the result was I became frustrated while he was probably satisfied with his learning as it progressed.

Not only did Robbie feel he could start using the machine before he knew all about it, and that he would learn about the machine by using it, but he also seemed to have the sense that the machine was there to obey his commands, a tool to help him achieve his intentions rather than an end in itself. The intimidated adult learner, on the other hand, seemed to have no such expectations, although she began developing them as she used the machine in the environment Newman had created. These examples strike me as another example of 'Who's in Charge Here?'. A comment from another of Newman's adult students provides an appropriate summary to this basic, introductory issue:

I found that it wasn't until I accepted the total responsibility for figuring out the system that I really discovered its true value. I had to discover the operations as a result of a need to use them and then I found my ability to interact with the text was much greater.

Learning, language development, and control

Why should the issue of control be an important theme for English educators? Psychologists, like Piaget, have shown how children primarily construct their own knowledge and intelligence, through a process of selecting specific data from the environment and generating hypotheses to explain the data. Further data may lead to their revising the hypotheses (or explanations), sometimes in radical ways. Children move through certain stages in their cognitive development, but they are the ones who direct themselves through the stages. They learn, by pursuing their own intentions, to solve the mysteries of their world. They create, and thus control, their own explanation of the world.

One of children's most powerful means for shaping their experience, structuring their knowledge, transforming the framework in the head is their personal language, since language use not only reflects our learning but also causes it. We know by structuring and we structure by uttering or writing.[1] Thus, much of children's learning results from conversational interaction with others in a collaborative meaning-making enterprise. In talking with parents, friends, and so on, children initiate, question, challenge, transform and confirm – all helpful strategies in learning. Significant others in children's lives usually play counterpart roles to the children's, essentially responding to what children are trying to do, assessing their hypotheses and responding to them, helping children achieve their intentions.[2] Using their language in this way is basically what causes their language ability to develop. In order to make and share new meaning (learning), children must find new ways of using language to structure that new meaning. All learning for children involves language development.[3]

An essential characteristic of my description of children's language and learning is their share of control of the processes, although they are obviously influenced in various ways by their interaction with others. The notion of children sharing in the control of their learning – its what, how, when, why, and with whom – has not only philosophical underpinnings (valuing independence and creativity in children), but theoretical ones as well.

This relationship of language and thought suggests that literacy ought not to be viewed as merely a technological or mechanistic process of decoding and encoding words in print. As Paulo Friere points out, any reading of the word is preceded by a critical, meaning-shaping reading of the world (which we can do by talking or by writing) and our reading of the word extends subsequently into a re-reading of the world. In other words, writing is a shaper, a 'reading' of our reality, and reading should be viewed as a critical rewriting of our understanding of reality. A mechanistic or behavioural notion of reading Friere calls 'walking on words' – as opposed to 'grasping their soul' (in press). Such a narrow view of reading is not limited to a skills approach to 'word-calling'. Even the more recent psycholinguistic focus in reading education[5] is based on an information-matching model of reading in which the text dominates and serves as ultimate criterion for a reader's meaning-making efforts. An alternative perspective involves a reader dialogizing on an equal footing with a text, going below the surface of a text to unveil its hidden assumptions and meanings, to confirm, revise, or reject its meaning as the reader tests out links with his or her experience, going beyond a text, to transcend meditatively any intended message in a text and to aesthetically create unique personal meaning for oneself.[6] In the same way, the only 'writing' which can be called 'authentic' is the free shaping of one's experience and knowledge through one's personal language[7], not the paraphrasing and direct copying which research shows makes up so much of the 'writing' in classrooms.[8]

The danger of a narrow view of literacy

The danger of treating literacy in a a narrow, mechanistic sense has been with us since long before computers were even invented. However, the use of computers in literacy instruction may increase that danger simply because computers are so good at the trivial aspects of literacy. With suitable software they can probably be more effective than teachers in teaching phonics, sight words, spelling, punctuation, and the other mechanical, or code, aspects of literacy. Even the best of the software falls short of treating literacy in a full, rich, critical sense. Recently I came across a software program, THE PUZZLER (see Miller and Burnett) designed to teach students how to predict their way through a passage, revising or confirming their predictions as they go along. The program had students stop at certain points in the passage to guess what certain aspects of the passage were about and then later to confirm or revise those predictions. As much of an advance as this program is over word-calling programs, it does not get beyond a factual, information-matching understanding of reading, in which the reader's comprehension is dominated by the text. We must ask, I believe, what such programs subtly teach children about reading. The answer to that question may have been provided already by the latest National Assessment of Educational Progress report in the US which indicates that in regard to literacy the nation's secondary school students are weakest in critical reading.[9] US educators have assumed that the findings reflect inherent deficits in the nation's pupils and are setting out with a vengeance to teach pupils critical thinking and reading 'skills' before they leave school. It seems equally plausible to me that the results indicate a deficit in school literacy programs and that pupils are merely learning well what school has taught them reading is.

The danger is that the increasing use of computers in literacy instruction will aggravate rather than relieve the problem.

The dangers of a controlling software

Of course, computer technology does not have to diminish, trivialise, or domesticate literacy. Some of its applications can empower learners and allow critical reading and writing.

As I look at computer hardware and software from the question of control of learning, I can place the technology in one of two camps – at least on the basis of its intent and potential. Much of what I would call 'skill and drill' software (which a large-scale 1983 survey by the Center for the Social Organization of Schools indicates makes up the great majority of the software used in US schools) is merely electronic worksheets. I agree that these 'high-tech' worksheets are empowered by computer technology in many ways: immediate response to the learner, recording and diagnosing of error patterns in pupil response, and so on. But note that the power flows to the teacher in these cases because the technology becomes an extension of the teacher, being present for him or her with the pupil, doing the teacher's clerical work, and so on. It is the student who must fit with the program's structure, to respond to the machines' initiative, to be evaluated by the machine. In effect, much of the interaction with the machine is just like the '*teacher initiates – pupil responds – teacher evaluates*' pattern of interaction that has been discovered in so many classrooms before the advent of computers. For example,

> *T:* Now, who can tell me what a disc jockey is? Brian?
> *P:* It's on the radio, the man who says what records are going to be played.
> *T:* Yes, good. On the radio. You get someone who announces the records and says 'Now, for Mrs Smith of 22 High Street, Easthampton'.[10]

Unfortunately computers are probably far more consistent and rigid in the pattern than any teacher could be.

Such an interaction frame, which characterizes both most computer software as well as most classroom interaction, indicates a highly directive teaching model which shares very little of the control of learning with pupils. As such, it contradicts the theoretical background I delineated earlier in this chapter. Research conducted across the English-speaking world, across grade/age levels, and across the curriculum[11] indicates greatly imbalanced roles, often mutually exclusive roles, between teachers and pupils. Teachers usually retain full rights to initiating, evaluating, explaining, and using extended language. Pupils, conversely, are often left to listen and to respond briefly, usually for purposes of publically displaying knowledge. Surveys suggest that pupils' writing is equally limited in quantity and in purpose.[12] Teacher responses to pupils' writing focus on correctness – correctness of the answer or of how the answer was stated.[13] Lunzer and Gardner discovered that 10–15-year-old average and above-average readers in Britain tended not to be critical, reflective readers since teachers placed so much emphasis on pupils providing the right answer from their reading.[14] Thus, pupils tended to give back to teachers the surface level of what they read. Right, of course, is defined by the teacher, textbook author, or other instructional authority. Edwards and Furlong have speculated that pupils may be forced in many classrooms to suspend their own world views in order to more easily see through the teacher's eyes.[15] As Douglas Barnes points out, we often expect children to arrive – in a learning sense – without having been given an opportunity to travel from their starting points.[16]

In such an educational environment, based on a 'top-down transmission' view of knowledge, it is not surprising to find (1) highly directive and controlling instructional patterns in most Language Arts software in use in schools and (2) a mechanistic, information-matching view of reading and writing embedded in that software. While there may be some place for some of that material, I must be concerned about learning environments that leave little room for pupils' use of personal knowledge as a base from which to learn, for pupils' exploratory language as a means of arriving at public knowledge, and for developing control, responsibility, and freedom in learning. The danger in the use of computers in literacy education is that they will fit too well into – and strengthen – classrooms that are already restrictive rather than elaborated language and learning environments.

Dangerous too is the *illusion*, for both pupils and teachers, that the learner is in control of the learning and the machine – turning it on and off, going back over certain portions, taking time with it, and so on. A colleague of mine, James Parsons, likens it to driving a train. You can slow down, speed up, even blow the train whistle. You think you are driving the train, but you can go only where the tracks are, and in that sense your course has been predetermined by someone else.

In the other camp, some technology has the potential to empower the pupils' learning efforts and outcomes. The emerging classic example, of course, is the word-processor. Early insight into the use of the machine indicates that it seems to facilitate the writing processes of many pupils (and adults too), merging the aspects of composing and revising more closely. The potential of the word-processor is enhanced because composing and revising are hardly 'just writing', but are basically coming to know – creating, structuring, and reshaping one's knowing. The word-processor also offers a potentially significant contribution to literacy in light of the rapidly growing body of work that suggests a writing road to reading or at least that the two sides of the literacy coin develop together symbiotically. Thus, we should view word-processing as developing pupils' reading as much as their writing, although the discussion about word-processing thus far has been almost entirely about writing.

The trivial aspects of literacy (which computers can deal with so well) do not necessarily all fall into my teacher-control camp. There are many code-oriented aspects of computer software with the potential to empower pupils in learning to read and write as well as in reading and writing to learn. Computer technology can enable young readers to keep personal lists of words for reading and spelling more easily and efficiently than the pre-floppy disc system of file cards in a box or sheets of paper. The self-editing capacities of some programs can relieve some of the time and drudgery of proof-reading. Error analysis programs for writing can aid a pupil in his or her own self-diagnosis of writing skills.

The key question for me is 'whom does the technology empower?' Generally, software that allows pupils to program, record, compose, and retrieve seems to have the potential for empowering learners, and for facilitating growth in authentic literacy. On the other hand, software that structures knowledge, including knowledge about literacy, in a particular way and leads pupils rather passively on a predetermined path through the material – and evaluates them in the same way – empowers teachers, giving them control not only over pupils' instruction but also over pupils' behaviour. Before the advent of 'drill and practice' software, many worksheets served the same purpose and what the reading and writing pupils did to complete them was primarily used to keep them quiet and busy in the classroom.[17] There is no less a danger of computers serving the same purpose.

The danger of a narrow view of knowledge and learning

The very limits of the technology create dangers. This is true even with regard to the computer's potential to empower pupils' learning and literacy. Just as any style of language has the power to shape our knowing, it simultaneously limits our knowing. Structuring knowing in one way automatically eliminates other possible structures or ways of knowing. Thus, to be creative, original, and continually learning, learners must be able to reshape and restructure existing knowledge as well as to acquire new knowledge. Computer language (not just the words, but also the sequences, frames, interaction patterns, and so on) both empowers and limits our knowing. We still know little about how it structures knowledge or the effect of such structuring on pupils. Many claims are made for the thinking processes that computers foster in learners, but on closer inspection 'thinking' usually refers to a linear, categorical, recursive, 'flow-chart' system of thought. In short, a highly 'logical' and rationalistic metaphor of knowing. Its potential appears to be in fostering growth as scientists and researchers in a narrow (but unfortunately typical) sense. While this type of thinking is undoubtedly valued in most classrooms, it is clear that such a view of the universe is only one way of knowing – and not necessarily the most powerful one. In addition, recent research indicates that such structuring of knowledge may be contrary, if not inimical, to children's ways of knowing.

Vygotsky has pointed out that the scientific concepts of schooling are structured in generalized, abstract, and impersonal modes, while the spontaneous concepts that learners play with as they make new sense are specific, concrete, and personal.[18] Language use or style, of course, is different for these two different ways of knowing. Other work, done largely in Britain, indicates that pupils shape their experience and transform new information they encounter primarily through language modes of narration and evaluation, while school shapes knowledge by modes such as classification. A classic example of the difference between these two metaphors of knowing and 'languaging' is offered in the following excerpt from a classroom discussion in a London secondary school which Dennis Searle recorded.[19] The class has been working in small groups on a task involving the notion of social classes. Caroline is having trouble fitting the information provided in class with her own experience and calls the teacher over.

Caroline:	Miss . . . Miss
Pupil A:	Social classes means upper classes right?
Observer:	Well all the classes are social classes together.
Pupil A:	Oh.
Observer:	You know.
Pupil A:	And the kind of school we go to?
Observer:	Yeh, what kind?
Pupil A:	We go to a social class school.
Observer:	Well every, what kind, what social class comes to this school?
Caroline:	Oh, middle class um.
Pupil A:	Do we . . .?
Caroline:	Middle, we are all middle class.
Pupil B:	I'm not, I'm poor.
Caroline:	You're middle class you [indistinct].
Pupil C:	We, we're working people.
Caroline:	I'm not, I'm not lower class.
Teacher:	I'll tell you what, it's a very difficult thing to talk . . .
Pupil A:	We're working class.
Teacher:	. . . about class because you can look at it from two different ways, well, lots of different ways, but two main ways. Firstly, how other people see you.
Caroline:	'Cause there's people worse than us.
Teacher:	Yes, it's not a question of better or worse so much. The main thing . . .

Caroline: I ain't working class.

Teacher: One of the things we talked about right, when we were looking at social class – you remember this guy I talked about, the registrar general? He has a list of different kinds of jobs that people do and by this list he puts people into different classes. So you have people like professors, the bowler hatters, businessmen, etcetera in the class number one, the upper class. In class two you get people like teachers, managers right in class two. In class three you get skilled manual workers and then you get unskilled manual workers. Now mainly it's certain kinds of [disruption]. That is he would tend to say that working class people normally have manual skilled jobs, unskilled, semi-skilled jobs or non-manual jobs right? But it can be that you have people from the working class that have very, very skilled jobs. Okay, it's a very, very rough, very crude definition.

Caroline: But we're still not working class.

Teacher: And as Caroline says, that a lot of it depends well on how you see your position in the class system.

Caroline: Maybe you are lower class, I'm not.

Teacher: All right?

Pupil: Yeh.

Caroline: I'm not.

Teacher: I mean it gets . . .

Caroline: We got a house so we can't be lower class.

Teacher: Well I haven't, but what does that make me?

Caroline: Peasant. (laughter)

While Caroline is stubbornly concrete, specific, and personally evaluative in her meaning-making, the teacher appears to be just as unidimensional in her mode of knowing – impersonal, generalized, and abstract. William Labov made much the same point about the differences in the language of schooling and the language of the street in his article 'The Logic of Non-Standard English'.[20] While we know little about language and learning in classrooms generally, we know even less about the structure of knowledge and style of language in computer software and how pupils interact with it in order to learn.

A highly rational and intellectual view of learning also raises the question of the place of the affective and the imaginative in learning. Reading and writing thrive particularly on the imaginative and emotional dimension. This excerpt from Maya Angelou's autobiography provides some insight to the richness possible in reading books.

I have tried often to search behind the sophistication of years for the enchantment I so easily found in those gifts. The essence escapes but its aura remains. To be allowed, no, invited, into the private lives of strangers, and to share their joys and fears, was a chance to exchange the Southern bitter wormwood for a cup of mead with Beowulf or a hot cup of tea and milk with Oliver Twist. When I said aloud, 'It is a far, far better thing that

I do, than I have ever done . . .' tears of love filled my eyes at my selfless-ness.[21]

Software which diminishes reading and writing to a purely cognitive, information-matching game can impoverish readers and writers. Note the experience of one adult user (Newman, 1984b) with the software package I referred to earlier, THE PUZZLER, and compare it with Angelou's description of her experience with books:

> Take, for example, the story The Dangerous Stuff. I predicted it could be an explosive, a drug, or some sort of magic potion. After reading the first page with its reference to 'a laboratory', 'experiments to help farmers and fishermen', and its being 'extremely dangerous to anything with two or four feet', I deleted drug and magic potion, retained explosive, and added 'some kind of chemical'. On page two I encountered such clues as 'It looks like muddy water', references to 'poking long poles into likely spots on the shores and in the beds of slow-moving streams and rivers', and of people and animals 'going in too easily'. I decided that an explosive no longer worked, and while uncomfortable about some kind of chemical, I decided to keep that prediction for the moment. Ah-ha, I said at the top of page three: 'The springs that help to form it can't been seen'. This is about some kind of geological formation – 'you can get sucked right in' – maybe quicksand. 'Your own weight makes you sink' – could be. Quicksand seemed to be confirmed on page four: 'it was ordinary sand that had had its grains pushed apart by water flowing up through, it'. I suspect there are other acceptable predictions, but my knowledge of land formations is limited and that was the response with which I was left.[22]

Newman's experience is undoubtedly *different* from Angelou's (even requiring a *different* writing style). The important question: is it a lesser one? These affective and aesthetic dimensions take on increased importance in light of Meek's work which suggests that the ability to let oneself have a rich literary (aesthetic) experience is vital in learning to read, even in the code-cracking sense.

A danger too, even in the technology that can empower users, is letting predetermined programs prevent the kind of powerful, intuitive leaps in understanding that mark milestones in learning for an individual or for a field of inquiry generally. Sir Bernard Lovell (1984), a radio astronomer and founder of Britain's Jodrell Bank Observatory, wonders as he looks at the field of radio astronomy, whether computers stifle creativity in scientists. While acknowledging the advantage of computers in effortlessly performing extremely complicated statistical interpretations of data to save time and yield new insights, he wonders about the absence of serendipitous and major new breakthroughs since the advent of computer applications in the field. We should perhaps wonder about the same possible danger with children and computers in school (as well as with restrictive, transmission classroom environments generally).

The social class dangers of computer use

Large-scale surveys of computer use in schools are alerting us to further dangers in their use; dangers which could be called social.

There is little doubt that literacy is power. Educational historians[24] and philosophers[25] have pointed out that literacy has basically belonged to social groups who enjoyed power and was officially or unofficially denied to the socially powerless. Literacy has been used as a tool by those in power to try to acculturate and socialize those out of the mainstream. Success in literacy has been closely linked with learners' degrees of acculturation and assimilation to the mainstream. It seems clear that computer literacy will be the new access to power in a high technology and information processing society. The computer's link with literacy may also reflect sociopolitical reality in society. What is uncertain yet is schooling's role in this distribution of power. For example, in some contexts, is has been reported that boys are enjoying greater access to computers than girls. (If so, it would be an ironic twist on the fact that girls in North American schools have historically enjoyed greater 'access' to and success with print literacy.)

Some disturbing observations have already been reported that schools in more affluent areas of the United States may be purchasing more computers and thus providing greater access to them for their pupils than schools in poorer areas. Also, pupils at these more affluent schools are more likely to enjoy exposure to microcomputers at home. Another large-scale survey, this time with California high school students[26], found a clear relationship between an assessment of pupils' computer literacy and parent educational level. Boys generally scored higher than girls, but the difference in scores between the highest and lowest parent education groups was three times as large as the difference between boys and girls.

It would be interesting to discover whether or not pupils' interaction with computers is different among pupils of varying socio-economic backgrounds. The question is prompted by other research which shows differing classroom interaction patterns in schools serving different socio-economic levels of society. Anyon (1981) discovered that pupils from contrasting social classes were exposed to different forms of teaching, based on different social relations and ideologies.[27] Pupils in working-class schools were primarily taught how to follow the rules for doing certain school work. As Anyon says, 'Work is often evaluated not according to whether it is right or wrong, but according to whether the children followed the right steps.[28] For pupils in a middle-class school, work was reduced to getting the right answer. Teachers in these schools raised questions designed simply to check the accuracy of answers, not to promote critical understanding of the answers or processes underlying them.

In the upper-class schools, pupils were engaged in a pedagogical process designed to develop their analytical prowess. Lessons were designed to promote critical reasoning, as well as leadership and management skills.

The best documented and perhaps most important finding about computer use in schools is how extremely limited it still is. Less than half the elementary schools in the US have a microcomputer.[29] The pupil–machine ratio in the province of British Columbia in Canada is 337:1.[30] Even more shocking is the fact that about 75% of US schools that own microcomputers leave them idle for over half the day and that 25% of schools use their computers for only one hour per day.[31]

My own three children attend a well-staffed and well-equipped elementary school, yet their access to computers in school can be measured in mere minutes per month – if that. It is quite clear that their exposure to computer use is far greater outside of school than it is in school. They help me conduct banking transactions by pushing buttons on the computer teller, they are familiar with electric digital numbers on gas pumps and manipulate those kinds of numbers as they set their wrist-watches. They understand in general terms how computers check out their books at the public library as well as record purchases at the supermarket by 'reading' bars of light. They either use or at least play with small calculators at home. Not only are they familiar with computers, but they see each use in a social and learning context of control, understanding, anxiety, and so on.

Despite large-scale and costly efforts, schools appear to be falling even further behind the uses of computers in society at large. Unless this situation changes, it may be that the computer–schooling link will develop as the link between electronic, visual media (film, television, videotapes, etc.) and schooling did. That is, the use of films and television became widespread through society before it appeared in school. Schools eventually picked up the use of these media in a minor way. Most children arrive at school visually 'literate' and school uses that ability of theirs but does little to challenge or develop it. Within the next few years, we may have most children arriving at school fairly computer literate, so that we can simply ask them to use that literacy in their learning without having to worry about developing it. Do we *want* that to be the case? If that does occur, pupils from more affluent backgrounds who have greater out-of-school access to microcomputers would enjoy an academic advantage. Working-class pupils would be at an even greater disadvantage in schools. Do we want *that* to be the case?

A final danger revealed by these large-scale surveys of the use of computers in schools is that the major use of computers in US schools is to teach computer literacy – separate from any other part of the curriculum. Perhaps educators are often forced into this approach because of the small numbers of computers available in school for so many children. In order to give all of them access to computers, perhaps all they can do is teach children how to operate the technology without using it in any kind of contextual application. Yet such an approach is akin to teaching how to use a pen, pencil, or typewriter but not how to use them for composing; or teaching kids how to use a calculator but never doing maths problems with it; or teaching brush techniques apart from actual painting. Turning computers into a subject unto themselves may work against pupils seeing them as means of empowering their learning, reading, and writing, but rather as something unrelated to reading and writing; in sum, to learning. It may also work against computers' powerful application to children's learning if viewed primarily as a code to crack. Computer literacy can be as narrow in conception as print literacy. The English education field has begun to view language, not as a separate subject matter, but as a means of learning and communication across the entire curriculum. Computers, too, make sense only across the curriculum, not apart from it, or tacked onto it.

The danger of ignorance and fear of computers

The dangers of computers enumerated so far are largely dangerous effects for *pupils* in school. *Educators*, too, must be aware of dangers for themselves with regard to computer use in school. There are several, I believe, all of which centre around the same issue of control that pupils face with computers.

The most prominent danger appears to be ignorance and fear about pupils' uses of computers on the part of many educators who don't understand or feel comfortable with computers themselves. Many educators feel pressure to rush into the purchase of computer hardware and software without adequate background knowledge to make intelligent choices. Many incidents have been reported of computers being purchased for schools and then being used improperly because teachers did not know how to use them – or even of teachers shunning their use because they did not understand, and thus feared, them. A report in a popular Canadian news magazine painted a disturbing picture. There is no doubt that personal computers are firmly entrenched in the Canadian educational system. But critics argue that the rush to computers has outstripped the ability of the system to use them. They cite poor teacher training, a shortage of sophisticated school-oriented software programs and, most important, the lack of clear overall computer strategies, as the prime reasons why the computer is in danger of becoming just an expensive toy in the schools. Commented Des Dixon, director of curriculum with the Ontario Teachers' Federation: 'We are definitely going somewhere with computers. The question remains: where?'.[32]

As English educators, we have a history of becoming anxious about new technology. The previous editor of the US Journal *Language Arts*, Julie Jensen, compiled a retrospective issue in January 1983 on the occasion of the journal's sixtieth anniversary. To do so, she read all the issues of the journal over the sixty years of its existence and compiled a 'scrapbook' edition of highlights. Jensen spoke at the NCTE annual convention in 1982 about the history of English education as she saw it in the pages of the journal. Much of her speech was in the form of multiple-choice questions for the audience. One such question was 'Which of the following technological advances did English educators feel would lead to the demise of literacy?': (a) computers, (b) television, (c) radio, (d) typewriters, (e) the ballpoint pen, (f) 'talkies'. The answer, of course (as was true for many of Jensen's questions), was 'All of the above'.

The danger of uncritical egocentricity

A further danger for us is that, as we ponder the educational issues about computers, pupils and literacy, we may settle for seeing through our own eyes, rather than through pupils' eyes, to try to understand these issues and reach conclusions about them.

The dangers I've portrayed in this chapter are not greatly different from what a number of other educators have been saying about computers and literacy. However, I have several concerns about this kind of analysis – even as I engage in it myself. My first concern is that we see too much through our own computer-fluent eyes and not enough through the eyes of computer learners. It's merely another version of the common story that few of us remember learning how to read and write and thus have trouble knowing what's involved for beginners. What may appear to be a rather simple plug-in worksheet on computer software involves a wide array of competencies of computer use from keyboard knowledge and screen reading to interaction frames and knowledge structure specific to computers. We often use the term 'computer literacy' but I doubt that we know yet what is truly involved in becoming computer literate. Is it learning certain interaction frames? Is it seeing the world through a binary framework? The research of Margaret Meek into conventional literacy among young readers may now tell us much about how to let pupils deal with computers and perhaps avoid creating remedial computer literates. And how do the competencies that make up computer literacy (whatever they are) compare with those which comprise print literacy (whatever they are)? One of the most basic questions we still face is 'What is literacy?' We must discover what the experience is for pupils, not settle for the adult-eye view, encapsulated explanations and theories that have been handed onto us and which uncritically we mouth.

Another danger of looking only through our own eyes is that we look at computers, rather than at children and computers. This tendency reminds me of much of the work with children's literature. Whether the literature is critiqued or reviewed, it is usually examined in itself, perhaps in historical or social context, but often in isolation from any context involving particular readers who give that literature a particular life and meaning. As a result, we still know very little about what happens when individual readers encounter individual books. The March issue of *Language Arts* each year has traditionally featured the theme of 'Children's Literature'. In my first year as editor, I changed it to 'Children and Literature' (a major shift, I think) and chose manuscripts which investigated a reader, a text, and the 'poem' (to use Rosenblatt's terminology[33]) resulting from that interaction. While I had literally scores of manuscripts on 'Children's Literature', I had only a small handful on 'Children and Literature'. My concern about that tendency now includes computers as they become a major topic in English education. I am receiving more and more manuscripts on computers in English education, but very few on computers and children in English education. The distinction is a major one and a worrisome one for me. We should be sceptical, I believe, of our ability as adult educators to predict or assume the nature of children's interactions with computers and the resulting outcomes of their computer learning simply by looking at computer programs, just as we should be sceptical of our ability to predict children's experiences with certain books by examining the books alone. I fear that we may soon have an official 'Computer Criticism' field to complement the existing Literary Criticism field. Such a stance may be helping to make computers a separate subject area in the school curriculum (like science, maths, history, etc.) rather than a learning tool and medium across the curriculum. The danger in a topic such as 'Computers and Literacy' is that we can forget that it implies 'Computer, Children and Literacy'.

If we wish to learn about the role of computers in child literacy and their effect on children's learning and 'languaging', we'll need to spend much time in classrooms with children and computers to study closely and carefully what happens there. Despite the amazing degree of interest in computers, I have found very little work describing and analysing what actually happens with them in classrooms, particularly from the sociopolitical context of language and learning I've used in my analysis in this chapter. Is it because such investigations are too costly in terms of time and money? Or is it like our stance toward children and literature, namely, that we think we don't need to study computers in use by children in social settings? I'd like to share one actual close-up study with you, reported by Bruce, Michaels, and Watson-Gegeo to indicate the power of insight with which it can provide us.

An elementary school in a low-income urban area of the US Northeast was celebrating Black History Week with a performance by and for the entire school. The show consisted of songs and skits in praise of famous black Americans and calling for racial harmony. One of the teachers, Mr Hodges, was Master of Ceremonies. One grade six teacher encouraged his students to write a critical review of the program on the classroom word-processor which used a program called QUILL. Many pupils were observed taking notes during the performance in preparation for their writing. They were to write a draft of the critique at their desk first, then have a conference with the teacher, and finally enter their writing on the computer. The teacher assigned the pupils numbers in order to manage access to the computer. The following is a copy of what one student entered on the computer.

'Black History Show'

Margaret Aponte

I liked the Black History show because I was supposed to see the little and big children singing so well and clearly.

The best acts were Mrs Martin's and Miss Simpson's classes. The songs were nice and the people on stage weren't scared.

The worst act was 'Famous Black People' – Mr Agosto's and Mr Anderson's class. Everybody messed up and forgot what to say, and they didn't speak clearly. They could have at least practiced more.

The scenery wasn't very much and the light was kind of dull, and the sound wasn't very good. Mr Hodges was speaking loud and clearly, and he was great on the stage. When the Glee-Club was singing so nice, Marines got very jealous and asked Mrs Evens to be in the Glee-Club. But when Mrs Evens said no she wrote bad things about the Glee-Club on the computer up-stairs.

But I really liked the Black History show. I gave it 3 stars because it was very good.

Briefly, the piece shows several characteristics of good writing (choice of words and order, overall beginning to end development, use of paragraphs employing description, contrast, etc., as organizing devices). However, the fourth paragraph seems incongruous in length, content, and linguistic form, especially the expression referring to Marines, a classmate. Margaret's writing appears to suffer a break-down or regression at that point. Without knowing the social writing context, we cannot interpret Margaret's writing well. Margaret's original, hand-written draft had only four paragraphs and the last paragraph read as follows:

The scenery was pretty good, and the light was bright enough, but the sound was not that good. Mr Hodges was speaking very loudly and was good on the stage. I think the show deserves three stars because it was very good.

Margaret was scheduled to enter her account on the computer just ahead of Marines and, while milling around near the machine waiting for their turns, Margaret read Marines' highly negative hand-written draft of her critique. Marines' sharpest criticism was for the Glee-Club. An excerpt:

> I don't know what happened to the Glee-Club, they were almost all weak.
> The audience couldn't hear them. They sounded soft then they went loud.
> It was a disaster!

When Margaret took her turn at the computer, she paused before entering the last sentence of her hand-written account, and composed the rest
of paragraph four and paragraph five directly on the computer. With this
insight, it is possible to understand Margaret's fourth paragraph (as well
as the cohesive device 'but' beginning her final paragraph) as an emotion-
ally-charged narrative, designed to discredit Marines as a critic. The
paragraph serves to enhance her own status as a critic in comparison to
her classmate. We also see her being affected by the more public nature
of the computer-assisted writing in this classroom.

   This type of 'close-up' investigation will tell us far more about children's learning with and through computers than any amount of what I
have termed 'computer criticism'. This particular example serves to bring
me directly back to my main, opening question: Who's in Charge Here?
Margaret's production of a piece of writing on a word-processor in the
particular context of classmates, teacher, and Black History Week
reminds us that this technology is being used by and for people living in a
sociopolitical context. Margaret used the computer to accomplish purposes in her life – to reflect upon herself, to define her relationship with
a classmate, as well as to complete an assignment. In this anecdote the
computer itself is not a major focus or issue. What *is* the focus or issue is
Margaret shaping her experience, using the computer as an extension of
herself.

   A final aspect of trying to see through pupils' eyes goes beyond the kind
of explanatory stance, which characterizes the incident with Margaret and
Marines, to what I might call the experiential stance of the question
'What's it like to be with a computer?' – for a particular individual, at a
particular time, for a particular task. Many of the concerns about computer use raised by critics have focused on this experiential aspect of being
with computers.

   Does working with a computer engender a sense of power or oppression? Is it characterized by social activity or solitude? Is it a personal or
impersonal experience? How does it influence and shape our coming to
know, our relating to other persons, the development of our humaneness?
These kinds of questions transcend our cause-and-effect model of
understanding language use (including language used through computers) as a tool or means. Instead, we begin to look at its very use as being
and becoming ourselves, as an experience that defines us and determines
for us what life is like. I have not yet been able to find examples of this kind
of insight, but a source of such possible insight is literature. Yet the image

of computers in literature is almost always an ominous one. How valid that perspective would be for all computer users remains to be seen. To answer the question we need to see through the eyes of real individuals, to feel with them, as they experience computers.

Some examples of the kind of insight I think we need come from autobiography. Here are several examples having to do with children and print, and aspects of what it was like to learn to read. The first comes from Jean-Paul Sartre's recollections of his early encounters with print and reading:

> Anne-Marie made me sit down in front of her, on my little chair; she leant over, lowered her eyelids and went to sleep. From this mask-like face issued a plaster voice. I grew bewildered: who was talking? about what? and to whom? My mother had disappeared, not a smile or trace of complicity. I was an exile. And then I did not recognize the language. Where did she get her confidence? After a moment, I realized: it was the book that was talking. Sentences emerged that frightened me: they were like real centipedes; they swarmed with syllables and letters, span out their diphthongs and made their double consonants hum; fluting, nasal, broken up with sighs and pauses, rich in unknown words, they were in love with themselves and their meanderings and had no time for me: sometimes they disappeared before I could understand them; at others, I had understood in advance and they went rolling on nobly towards their end without sparing me a comma. These words were obviously not meant for me.[35]

A second example comes from Richard Rodriguez's autobiography:

> Reading was, at best, only a chore. I needed to look up whole paragraphs of words in a dictionary. Lines of type were dizzying, the eye having to move slowly across the page, then down, and across . . . The sentences of the first books I read were coolly impersonal. Toned hard. What most bothered me, however, was the isolation reading required. To console myself for the loneliness I'd feel when I read, I tried reading in a very soft voice. Until: 'Who is doing all that talking to his neigbour?' Shortly after, remedial reading classes were arranged for me with a very old nun.
>
> At the end of each school day, for nearly six months, I would meet with her in the tiny room that served as the school's library but was actually only a storeroom for used textbooks and a vast collection of *National Geographics*. Everything about our sessions pleased me: the smallness of the room; the noise of the janitor's broom hitting the edge of the long hallway outside the door; the green of the sun, lighting the wall; and the old woman's face blurred white with a beard. Most of the time we took turns. I began with my elementary text. Sentences of astonishing simplicity seemed to me lifeless and drab: 'The boys ran from the rain . . . She wanted to sing . . . The kite rose in the blue'. Then the old nun would read from her favourite books, usually biographies of early American presidents. Playfully she ran through complex sentences, calling the words alive with her voice, making it seem that the author somehow was speaking directly to

me. I smiled just to listen to her. I saw there and sensed for the very first time some possibility of fellowship between a reader and a writer, a communication, never *intimate* like that I heard spoken words at home convey, but one nonetheless *personal*.[36]

As you can see, such 'literary' insight structures *our* knowing differently than a scientific, rationalist orientation does. It can free us from looking and knowing in only one way. As English educators, we claim to be humanists. Perhaps our learning about 'computers, pupils and literacy' requires that we develop the eye of the poet or artist as much as the eye of the psychologist or sociologist. Unfortunately, we have not done it yet. The danger is that we may never do it, seduced by our belief that we can understand what it's like by looking at computers, not at children.

The danger of treating computers as a special issue

A final danger, one implied in much of what I have already said, and perhaps the greatest danger, is that we think of computers as a completely new educational issue. Most of the dangers pointed out so far are dangers that existed before computers made their way into the classroom. While not denying the new technical experience and potential that computers offer, I have concluded that the basic issues outlined regarding their use are human issues rather than technological issues. While computers may empower users in new ways for literacy, most decisions made about the purchase and use of the software reflect teachers's understanding of reading and writing and their belief in how it is learned. The interaction frames, between the machine and the learner, reflect present oral and written interaction in classrooms, not solely because of limitations of the technology, but in large part because it reflects the understanding and expectations of many educators about the nature of teaching.

While we can't be sure because it was not directly studied, it seems that Margaret's teacher chose the kind of computer program he did because it reflected his beliefs and attitudes about learning, language use and classroom interaction. Obviously most other North American teachers do not share the same beliefs and understandings since they choose drill and skill computer software. I do not doubt that, if computer technology did not exist, those teachers would create much the same kind of environments and interaction patterns, structuring knowledge in certain ways in their classrooms.

Pupils will naturally approach computers with a sense of being in control of them, of being empowered by them, *if* the students are already in classroom, home or community environments that have fostered in them a sense of direction and control over their own lives and learning. They will view machines in the same way that they view their own natural language use, as Polanyi says, as extensions of themselves:

I have shown how our subsidiary awareness of our body is extended to include a stick, when we feel our way by means of the stick. To use language in speech, reading, and writing is to extend our bodily equipment and become intelligent human beings. We may say that when we learn to use language, or a probe, or a tool, and thus make ourselves aware of these things as we are of our bodies, we *interiorize* these things and *make ourselves dwell in them*. Such extensions of ourselves develop new facilities in us.[37]

If pupils have not been in those kinds of environments, they may well feel shaped and controlled by computer use, as, I'm afraid, many pupils feel currently about reading and writing as a result of their instructional experiences with them. And, of course, the same provision applies to us educators as well.

A large-scale study in the United States that was reported in the mass media linked the heavy, addictive use of computers by husbands (note, not wives) to marriage break-up. Further investigation discovered that these husbands found it easier to deal with an infinitely logical, infinitely patient, infinitely consistent computer than with real persons, such as their wives. We could blame computers for the marriage break-ups, but that would be attacking the symptom, not the cause which lies in the personalities of the husbands in the study, and their inability to cope with relationships. (As a colleague of mine wondered aloud, 'Is a computer the perfect gift for the man who has no-one?')

The same problem affects research design and interpretations of studies that seek to determine the computer's *effect* on students in some way apart from any consideration of the social and learning context in a classroom. For example, some studies have discovered that computer use appears to increase social interaction and collaborative effort in a class-room. Yet other work, including some by my own students, indicates otherwise. The difference in outcomes in studies like these are partly determined at least by the classroom environment in which the computer exists, which groupings of pupils use it, and so on. As we investigate computer use in classrooms we must remember that it cannot be acontextual, asocial, or apolitical.

Conclusion – or beginning?

At this point, I hope that you feel like Robert Frost as he wrote: 'Two roads diverged in a yellow wood'. ('The Road Not Taken') For while this chapter has dealt explicitly with a path filled with the dangers that I perceive with the use of computers, I hope that by so doing it has also pointed out a path of potential benefits. We must first be critically aware of the two paths. But then, like Frost, we can choose which one we follow. We can decide who's in charge here:

> Two roads diverged in a wood, and I – I took the one less travelled by, and that has made all the difference.[38]

8 The Future of Literacy

STEPHEN MARCUS

We began this book by referring to Plato's attitude to writing. He wrote that it 'destroys memory [and] weakens the mind', and that it is 'an inhuman thing'. The point was made that this is a common attitude toward the computer, and this is particularly so with teachers of English and the Language Arts, who are more likely to consider the computer as a distrusted intruder rather than as a helpful ally in situations where creativity, intuition, and humane sensibilities are of paramount concern.

Media analyst Neil Postman has noted that there are important consequences of changing the form of information, its quantity, speed or direction of flow. The widespread use of writing did, indeed, affect expectations for, and ability to use, human memory. But did writing – a high-technology development from Plato's perspective – dehumanize us? What are we to do then, with Seymour Papert's assertion that children can learn to write at the same time they learn to speak? Are those of us involved with computer-assisted writing instruction unwitting accomplices to childhood's end?

The future of literacy – that is, the nature and proficiency of reading and writing skills – is as problematic now as it has been in the past. As computers are being transformed from mere data- and word-processors to knowledge and idea processors, they are providing new and increasingly rich environments that both enhance and transform our own capacities. Earlier chapters in this book have described some of the initial attempts to shape and manage this transformation. This final chapter will attempt to provide some frameworks for consolidating what we know of past developments and current trends. In addition, questions for future inquiry will be outlined, in hopes of providing guidance, not for defining and predicting the future, but for describing the *manner* in which it is being shaped.

The general orientation for this chapter is derived from John Naisbitt's book, *Megatrends*.[1] He deals there with large-scale transformations in society that are 'already changing our inner and outer lives'. The specific trends Naisbitt identifies are not central to our concerns here. What are important are his attitude and method. He is interested in those 'larger patterns [that are] not always clear . . . [It is] only by understanding the larger patterns [that] the individual events begin to makes sense'. Formulating a framework that describes these patterns sensitizes us to our environment and provides us with a set of terms for talking about what we see happening. Naisbitt, who is in the trend-analysis business, uses his analyses to provide 'a framework into which I mentally sort all of the other information I come across'.

The following discussion risks oversimplifying a very complex web of technological advances. The real point is not to predict the specific picture of the future but to provide structures for making sense of the world of computer-assisted education and its impact on literacy.

Unto the fifth generation

One way to consider past, present and future developments of computer use in the Language Arts is to think of 'generations', a term which has parallels in the field of hardware development. With regard to the computer-assisted teaching of writing, for example, there can be identified five such stages:

- Drill and practice
- Writer aids
- Author systems
- Idea processors
- Publishing systems

A brief overview of each of these generations will provide a useful organizing framework for much of what has been discussed in previous chapters and will prepare the way for considerations to be addressed later.

Drill and practice was the earliest (because easiest) application of computers to writing instruction. Unfortunately, in its least successful, albeit widespread form, this amounted to 'finding better ways to burn witches'. That is, people took activities that did bad things to students and used computers to do a more *efficient* job of doing bad things to them. In addition, it was in this area that (even today) some of the most questionable aspects of video arcade games have found their way into educational software (e.g. gender bias in graphics and in reliance on competitive aggression). As software designers have incorporated more instructional savvy – for example, not rewarding wrong answers with more exciting and interesting results than right answers received – and as better diagnostic and score management systems have been incorporated into the software, these first-generation applications have taken a respectable, if limited, place in the courseware available for helping students improve their writing skills.

First-generation software will undoubtedly continue to improve in quality. However, it is with the introduction of second-generation software that the computer begins to have a more profound affect on the composing process. These *writer aids* focus on one or the other stage of the composing process: prewriting, or writing, or rewriting.

Several useful approaches to computer-asssisted prewriting allow students to generate preliminary ideas and structures for literary analysis, expository essays, poems, etc. In general, the computer presents the student with a coherent set of questions modelled on those which a teacher might use to elicit the students' own ideas or to suggest perspectives that may help the writers take a broader or more creative approach to the topic at hand.

A different kind of computer-assisted prewriting – one that doesn't require specialized software – demonstrates one of the unique qualities of the technology itself. This technique is called 'invisible writing with computers'. Simply by completely turning down the monitor's screen brightness, students are prevented from seeing their prewriting even though their evolving texts are being recorded by the word-processor. (They eventually, of course, brighten the display to see and work on what they've written.) Students have reported that invisible writing helped them concentrate on their ideas rather than get distracted with compulsive and premature proofreading. It also produced writing that 'came more from within' themselves and helped them 'understand that writing really begins with prewriting'.

This is a simple trick to play with the computer, yet it suggests how word-processors themselves have *instructional* dimensions. They teach students that writing isn't what it used to be: excruciating preparation for tedious revision and re-typing. Students see that their words are no longer 'carved in stone'. They are, instead, written in light. The students are engaged in a more fluid, plastic, or flexible medium that offers little resistance to physical manipulation.

Second-generation software, in addition to prewriting programs and writing tools like word-processors *per se*, includes programs that will analyse the surface features of the student's text and provide information on such dimensions as the degree of sexist language, jargon, or imprecise diction. Analyses may also include information about the degree of nominalization or of selected parts of speech. Various programs will check spelling and punctuation. Especially sophisticated software may check on subject-verb agreement and use of active versus passive voice. An ever-increasing number of programs will suggest changes and will provide direct instruction to help students make appropriate revisions.

It should be remembered that second-generation software focuses on a single stage of the composing process. The prewriting software has virtually no word-processing capability. Word-processors may help you to search-and-replace, but they won't help you to figure out what to put there in the first place. Many text analysers will dutifully help you to adjust the readability of any garbage you type in, but they won't help you to avoid delivering that first load of trash.

More instructionally rich second-generation software is being designed, and there will always be a place for it. It was inevitable, however, that there would be developed software that combined capacities for pre-writing, writing, and rewriting. Such *author systems* (like QUILL, WAN-DAH, WRITER'S HELPER, and WRITER'S WORKSHOP, in the US) provide direct instruction in prewriting, include a word-processor, and have editing and rewriting aids. Such systems attempt to replicate selected portions of student–teacher interaction during the development of a piece of writing. They are analogous to attempts in other areas to develop that class of computer-assisted problem-solving tools known as 'expert systems'.

Author systems represent a useful advance over the single-purpose approach of writer aids. There is also, however, a fourth generation of software which takes a different approach to collaborating with a writer. These *idea processors* attempt to actively manipulate text based on its content, not merely on the basis of surface characteristics of combinations of letters and punctuation. A program like THINK TANK structures knowledge and topics in traditional outlining schema. MAXTHINK, based on the thinking-skills approach of Edward De Bono, includes commands to help writers synthesize, form and cross boundaries of relationships, establish priorities of ideas, etc. Related systems, like THOR and THOUGHT PROCESSOR also attempt to mirror and assist the user's conceptualizing abilities.

Not all these kinds of idea processors provide the integrated prewriting, writing and rewriting functions characteristic of third-generation systems. They might, perhaps, be re-categorized as a different, more sophisticated kind of second-generation software. Nevertheless, they represent enough of a conceptual advance to be usefully considered as the first attempts in a class by themselves.

The notion of fifth-generation software, *publishing systems*, moves us from the domain of the available to that of the probable. That is, the pieces of such systems are currently in use and are in some situations combined to varying degrees. At the present time one can only extrapolate from current hardware and software in order to picture what complete systems would most likely provide.

A publishing system will, first of all, most certainly contain the kinds of integrated systems already described but in more sophisticated versions. That is, there will be interactive components to help writers discover, invent and give order to their ideas. There will be word-processors and text analysers to help record, diagnose, assess and revise the writer's work.

In addition, however, there will be facilities, notably through telecommunications devices and software, for writers to get responses from human readers prior to and following publication. And 'publication' itself will take varying forms in both 'on-line' versions and 'hardcopy' versions.

Computers already allow groups of people easy access to each other's work and allow teachers to examine the various drafts of a student's composition without taking the work away from the writer. Many teachers have developed informal ways to have comments added to students' word-processing files, and specially developed software already exists that allows teachers to 'mark up' disc files.

In addition to these more traditional, institutional, approaches, there is the growing availability of electronic bulletin boards, computer-based conference systems, and database networks. These are more and more being designed to provide students the opportunity to write to others and get real responses from real readers (i.e., not computer analyses) who may be less likely to belong to the same cultural milieu as the writer. One striking example of this is the work headed by James Levin at the University of California, San Diego. For some years he has arranged for children in southern California to correspond with children in Alaska, using specialized second-generation and telecommunications software. Students have experienced the fascination and frustration of trying to make themselves clear. Computer-assistance in this case increases the speed and helps shape the structure of their correspondence. It enhances a dimension of the composing process that writing teachers have long understood to be a crucial, although often neglected, part of the writing curriculum: writing for a real audience. As informal as such 'publication' is, it helps a great deal in encouraging students to take their own and others' writing seriously.

There is another growing trend in consumer (as opposed to commercial) software and that is the availability of easy-to-use graphics software that allows people to *design* their text, i.e., to mix text and graphic images, to mix type fonts (including Old English and fanciful fonts), to modify the appearance of letters by outlining and shadowing letter forms, etc. One software package, THE PRINT SHOP, lets the user create fanciful letterhead stationery, greeting cards, posters, and banners.

Such graphics utilities not only encourage the development of *visual* literacy, they also allow students to produce personally designed and specialized writing materials. They increase the likelihood that students will want to produce, display and 'publish' their writing. Where the constructing of personalized databases and interactive fiction/adventure stories develops students' skills as 'information architects', such image-processing software encourages and develops students' skills as 'information artists'.

And yet, as many advances as there have been in computer-assisted writing instruction, it is well to remember that – 'generations' not-withstanding – the field is in its infancy. Well-intentioned software developers have been trying their best to 'computerize' various aspects of the composing process, with more or less success. At this point, their willingness to experiment and to explore is perhaps the most hopeful sign.

There is hardly agreement on the best ways to teach writing itself – let alone with computer assistance. The field is fortunate to have plenty of good models to choose from in the instructional arena and exciting development tools to adopt from the technological domain. Most important, however, is that very talented teachers are combining the best of both worlds to the benefit of themselves and their students.

Predicting the future

The question still remains: How will literacy be affected by the new technology? The preceding section described some of the changes in the *technology*, but said precious little about what real difference these would make in the definitions of reading and writing, or in their teaching, or in their acquisition.

It is commonplace wisdom that when predicting the future, it's safe to specify either what or when, but never both. It's hard, though, to resist a bit of prognostication. A 'Delphi study'[2] currently being conducted by Barber and LaConte at the University of Connecticut is attempting to identify changes (either positive or negative) in the teaching of English that might occur during the next fifteen years that will result in the impact of technology on society and/or the schools. It's safe to say that by the end of the study the final list will be different from any of the first ones attempted. Here, however, is one such initial list:

- More education will be done in the home through instructional databases and networks. These will be provided by commercial sources, not educational institutions.
- Publishing systems of the kind already described will replace the typewriter as the major composing tool.
- Interactive reading and writing software will define new genres for creative writers and critics alike.
- Software which generates its own text will change the nature of writer-text-reader relationships, particularly in the case of formulaic writing.
- Spelling and style checkers will make it even harder to convince students to learn many of the basic skills.
- Student papers will become more like illuminated manuscripts and

will contain more icons and pictographs. Teachers will have to figure out how to read and assess such work.

- Grading will become more dependent on the kind of data available from style checkers.
- Handwriting will degenerate for more students; in general, it will develop as one of the fine or applied arts.
- Ease of personal publication (hardcopy or on software networks) will change the value of 'getting published' and will affect standards of assessment for published work.
- Writing labs will become like studio art courses, in which instructors can monitor and give instant advice on students' writing.

Readers may want to omit or add certain items – as well they should. It is, in fact, less important whether such predictions are accurate than that by a concentrated effort to articulate them, they aid the novice oracle in focusing attention and insight to a problematic but fascinating field.

There also remains the problem of *how* to focus attention, how to structure our reading of current events and developing trends. One set of guidelines may be adapted from the work of two Stanford University researchers, William Paisley and Milton Chen. They have provided a seminal report on 'Children and Electronic Text: Challenges and Opportunities of the "New Literacy" '. Their study was of four different but related technologies: teletext, videotext, interactive cable television and microcomputers. It provides an extremely useful framework for organizing and understanding the developments we see reported everywhere, including those from newspapers, from teacher training centre newsletters, from professional journals, and from our everyday experience.

It is important to realize, as these authors point out, that we know 'as little about [the effects of this new technology on literacy] as we knew about the effects of television in 1955'. It is expected that the new technologies will transform, not merely supplement, students' learning. Also, the nature of the specific technologies is expected to continue changing at a disconcerting rate. (Television technology, by way of contrast, changed little over a quarter-century.)

Paisley and Chen frame a series of questions about the effects of present and future technologies on literacy. Their overall question is this:

Who learns what from which electronic text system and with what effects on other learning and behaviour, and when does this all take place?

On the basis of their discussion, it is possible to consolidate their discussion into groups of questions to help us see the larger patterns – demographic, psychological, sociological. We can use these questions to help ourselves become Naisbitt-like trend analysts, to develop our personal frameworks to enable us to 'sort out and assess today's events', whether local or national, and perhaps will enable us to shape future conditions.

Identifying trends in computers and literacy
(After Paisley and Chen, 'Children and Electronic Text')

Who?
Which socioeconomic groups are acquiring access to the systems? In what gender ratios? What barriers are present and how are they being overcome? Which groups are making use of public access systems (including those in libraries and museums)? Within social groups, what are the social roles and personality types of those making greater or less use of the systems?

Learns what?
What content sources are available and which ones are actually being used? What levels of learning are being attained? What *kinds* of learning? What benefits are being derived from casual versus directed use of the systems? What are the unintended learning outcomes being reported?

From which electronic text system?
Are different kinds of groups or individuals tending to use particular text systems? Which systems are reaching limits inherent in their technologies? Are some systems showing increasing potential?

With what effects on other learning?
Are electronic text systems reinforcing or conflicting with other modes of learning? (For example, are students coming to expect a teacher to have 'pause', 'review' or 'fast forward' functions?) Are children who use electronic text systems extensively characterized as having poorer or richer home and school experiences otherwise?

With what effects on behaviour?
How are electronic text systems affecting students' personal adjustment, social development or patterns of interaction with other students and adults?

In what temporal frame of reference?
Are the questions above being asked at the time of the students' initial or later use of the technology? And is the technology itself in its early or mature state of development?

This is a substantial and perhaps daunting set of questions, not all of which will be relevant to a given situation. They do provide, though, the kind of consolidating device that helps bring order to a wealth of disparate reports. Consider, for example, just these few instances (related to the US):

- Futurists predict that, by 1990, ten million people will be 'telecommuting'; i.e., earning a living in their own homes using telecommunication devices.
- Source Telecomputing Corporation is entering the education market in a national programme and plans to offer local, statewide, and national networking through which educators at various levels can exchange information, have access to a variety of computerized courses and archival information, and obtain reviews of hardware and software.
- Futurists predict that before the end of the century, 50% of all software will be either for or from telecommunications sources. Interactive videogames and educational software (for adults as well as children) will be a close second.
- 'In most fields, anyway, scholarly publishing and communication will have moved to a paperless, computerized mode, and university administrators will shake their heads in wonder at the antiquated humanists who insist that a large share of the library's resources be spent on books and magazines so clearly doomed to physical extinction'.[3]

In each of these examples, someone is reporting or predicting developments which will have profound effects on student and adult literacy – its acquisition or practice. Clearly, we live in a time of ungovernable and uncertain transition. And with this kind of uncertainty comes a predictable kind of retrenching. In the United States, the editors of *Educational Technology* (August 1984) are already noting that 'It has taken longer than usual for the critics to begin to pummel this particular innovation in the schools, but now the backlash against computers in education has begun'.

If anything can be predicted about computers and literacy with much assurance, it is that some people will oversell the technology as a positive force and that others will decry it as an abomination. Perhaps the most we can hope for (and it has always served us well) is a continued reliance on talented teachers acquiring an informed exuberance. As always, they will be a major force in making the most of whatever the technology and their students offer them.

Appendix 1
Related Reading

A Books and booklets

Adams, Anthony and Esmor Jones *Teaching Humanities in the Microelectronic Age* (Open University Press, Milton Keynes, 1983)

Centre for the Teaching of Reading *Computer Software for Primary Language Work* (Centre for the Teaching of Reading, University of Reading, Berkshire, 1984)

Chandler, Daniel *Micro-Primer Study Text* (Tecmedia, on behalf of the Microelectronics Education Programme, Loughborough, Leicestershire, 1982)

Chandler, Daniel (ed.) *Exploring English with Microcomputers* (Council for Educational Technology, in association with NATE, on behalf of the Microelectronics Education Programme, London, 1983)

Chandler, Daniel *Young Learners and the Microcomputer* (Open University Press, Milton Keynes, 1984)

Daiute, Colette *Computers and Writing* (Addison-Wesley, Reading, Mass., in press)

Davies, Graham *Computers, Language and Language Learning* (Information Guide 22, Centre for Information on Language Teaching and Research, London, 1982)

Geoffrion, Leo D., and Olga P. Geoffrion *Computers and Reading Instruction* (Addison-Wesley, Reading, Mass., 1983)

Higgins, John (ed.) *Computers and English Language Teaching* (British Council Inputs, British Council, 1982)

Higgins, John and Tim Johns *Computers and Language Learning* (Collins Educational, London, 1984)

Hills, Philip *The Future of the Printed Word* (Open University Press, Milton Keynes, 1980)

Kolers, P., M. Wrolstad and H. Bouma (eds.) *Processing of Visible Language*, 2 Vols. (Plenum Press, 1979/1980)

Lathrop, Ann and Bobby Goodson *Courseware in the Classroom: Selecting, Organizing and Using Educational Software* (Addison-Wesley, Menlo Park, Calif., 1983)

Lawlor, Joseph (ed.) *Computers in Composition Instruction* (SWRL Educational Research and Development, Los Alamos, Calif., 1982)

Mason, George E., Jay S. Blanchard, and Danny B. Daniel *Computer Applications in Reading* (International Reading Association, Newark, Delaware, 1983)

Mcluhan, Marshall *Understanding Media – The Extensions of Man* (McGraw-Hill, 1964)

Moore, Phil *Computers and English: A Practical Guide* (Methuen, in press)
Mowshowitz, Abbe *Inside Information: Computers in Fiction* (Addison-Wesley, Reading, Mass., 1977)
National Council of Teachers of English *Guidelines for Software Review and Evaluation* (Urbana, Illinois, NCTE, undated)
Northeast Regional Exchange *Teaching Writing Through Technology – A Resource Guide* (Northeast Regional Exchange, Chelmsford, Mass., 1983)
Papert, Seymour *Mindstorms – Children, Computers and Powerful Ideas* (Basic Books, New York, 1980; Harvester Press, Brighton, Sussex, 1980)
Postman, Neil *The Disappearance of Childhood* (W. H. Allen, London, 1983)
Robinson, Brent *Microcomputers and the Language Arts* (Open University Press, Milton Keynes, in press)
Standiford, Sally N., Kathleen Jaycox and Anne Auten *Computers in the English Classroom: A Primer for Teachers* (ERIC/NCTE, Urbana, Illinois, 1983)
Sharples, Mike *Cognition, Computers and Creative Writing* (unpublished PhD thesis, University of Edinburgh, 1983)
Shostak, Robert (ed.) *Computers in Composition Instruction* (International Council for Computers in Education, Eugene, Oregon, 1984)
Walker, Decker F., and Robert D. Hess *Instructional Software: Principles and Perspectives for Design and Use* (Wadsworth, Belmont, Calif., 1984)
Wresch, William (ed.) *The Computer in Composition Instruction* (National Council of Teachers of English, Urbana, Illinois, 1984)

B   Articles

Appleby, Bruce, 'Computers and Composition: An Overview' in *Focus*, 9, 3, Spring 1983
Bradley, Virginia, 'Improving Students' Writing with Microcomputers' in *Language Arts* 59, 7, October 1982
Chandler, Daniel, 'Are we still living in Lagado?', *Bluefile 1* (Microelectronics Education Programme, Newcastle, 1981)
Chandler, Daniel, 'The Games Some Pupils Play' in *Educational Computing*, November 1981, p. 28
Chandler, Daniel, 'The Potential of the Microcomputer in the English Classroom' in Anthony Adams (ed.), *New Directions in English Teaching* (Falmer Press, Lewes, Sussex, 1982)
Chandler, Daniel, 'Great Expectations' in *Educational Computing*, November 1982, pp. 24–25
Chandler, Daniel and Rose, 'Hands up for Hands on' in *Times Educational Supplement*, 1 July 1983, p. 40
Chandler, Daniel, 'Microcomputers and the English Teacher' in Colin Terry (ed.) *Using Microcomputers in Schools* (Croom Helm, 1984)
Chandler, Daniel, 'Conscious Change: Technology and Creativity' in *Times Educational Supplement*, 25 May 1984, p. 40
Chandler, Daniel, 'An Antidote to Infomania' in Ann Irving (ed.) *Infostorms* (Harper and Row, London, 1984)

Clark, Michael, 'Microwriters in School', *NORIC Newsletter 2* and *3*, Summer/ Autumn 1983, MEP Northern Regional Information Centre, Newcastle-upon-Tyne.

Clements, Douglas H., 'The ABC's and Beyond: Computers, Language Arts, and the Young Child' in *Computers, Reading and the Language Arts* 1, 3, Winter 1983, pp. 15–18

Collins, Allan, Bertram C. Bruce and Andee Rubin, 'Microcomputer-Based Writing Activities for the Upper Elementary Grades' in *Proceedings of the Fourth International Learning Technology Congress and Exposition* (Society for Applied Learning Technology, Orlando, Florida, 1982)

Collins, Allan, 'Teaching Reading and Writing with Personal Computers' in J. Oransano (ed.), *A Decade of Reading Research: Implications for Practice* (Erlbaum, Hillsdale, New Jersey, 1984)

Daiute, Colette, 'Writing, Creativity and Change' in *Childhood Education*, March/April 1983, pp. 227–31

Edelsky, Carole, 'The Content of Language Arts Software: A Criticism' in *Computers, Reading and Language Arts* 1, 4, Spring 1984, pp. 8–11

Frederiksen, John, Beth Warren, Helen Gillotte and Phyllis Weaver, 'The Name of the Game is Literacy' in *Classroom Computer News*, May/June 1982, pp. 23–27

Govier, Heather, 'Primary Language Development' in *Acorn User*, May 1983, pp. 45–51

Harrison, Colin, 'The Textbook as an Endangered Species: the implications of economic decline and technological advance on the place of reading in learning' in *Oxford Review of Education* 7, 3 (1981), pp. 231–40

Hawkins, Jan, Karen Sheingold, Maryl Gearhart and Chana Berger, *Microcomputers in Schools: Impact on the Social Life of Elementary Classrooms* (Center for Children and Technology, Bank Street College of Education, New York, 1982)

High, Julie and Carol Fox, 'Seven-year-olds discover Microwriters', *English in Education* 18, 2, Summer 1984, pp. 15–25

Johns, Tim, 'The Uses of an Analytic Generator: The Computer as Teacher of English for Specific Purposes', English for Overseas Students Unit, Department of English Language and Literature, University of Birmingham

Johns, Tim, 'The Computer and English for Special Purposes', English for Overseas Students Unit, Department of English Language and Literature, University of Birmingham

Kleiman, Glenn and Mary Humphrey, 'Word-Processing in the Classroom' in *Compute!*, Issue 22, March 1982, pp. 96–99

Lawler, Robert, 'One Child's Learning: Introducing Writing with a Computer', AI Memo No 575, Logo Memo No 56, Artificial Intelligence Laboratory, Massachusetts Institute of Technology, March 1980

Leibowicz, J., 'CAI in English' in *English Education*, 14, 4, December 1982

Lovell, Sir Bernard, 'Do Computers Stifle Creativity?' in *Science Digest*, June 1984, p. 94

Macdonald, Nina, 'Pattern Matching and Language Analysis as Editing Supports', Bell Laboratories, Piscataway, New Jersey

Marcus, Stephen, 'Compupoem: A Computer-Assisted Writing Activity' in

English Journal, February 1982a, pp. 96–99

Marcus, Stephen, 'Compupoem: CAI for Writing and Studying Poetry' in *The Computing Teacher*, March 1982b, pp. 28–31

Marcus, Stephen, 'The Muse and the Machine: A Computers and Poetry Project' in *Classroom Computer News* 3, 2, November/December 1982, pp. 28–31

Marcus, Stephen and Sheridan Blau, 'Not Seeing is Relieving: Invisible Writing with Computers' in *Educational Technology*, April 1983, pp. 12–15

Marcus, Stephen, 'Sexism and CAI' in *Computers, Reading and Language Arts*, Fall 1983, p. 6

Marcus, Stephen, 'Childhood's End' in *Computers, Reading and Language Arts*, Spring 1983, p. 7 ff.

Marcus, Stephen, 'Computers in the Curriculum: Writing' in *Electronic Learning*, October 1984, p. 54 *ff.*

Miller, L. and J. D. Burnett, 'The PUZZLER: Reading Strategy Lessons in a Computer-Based Mode', Reading-Canada lecture (in press)

Newman, J., 'Language Learning and Computers' in *Language Arts* 60 (1984a), pp. 494–97

Newman, J., 'Online: Reading, Writing and Computers' in *Language Arts* 61 (1984b), pp. 867–72

Newman, J., 'Online: Some Reflections on Learning and Computers' in *Language Arts* 61 (1984c), pp. 414–47

O'Donnell, H., 'Computer-Assisted Instruction in the English Classroom', ERIC/RCS Resource Packet, ERIC Clearinghouse on Reading and Communication Skills, 1981

Robinson, Brent, 'A Linguistic Perspective on the Interaction of Computer and Human in an Educational Context', November 1981. Unpublished but available from the author at the Department of Education, University of Cambridge

Robinson, Brent, 'Fiction and the New Electronic Media', Faculty of Educational Studies, University of Southampton, May 1982

Robinson, Brent, 'Reading and the Video Screen', *Media in Education Research, No. 2*, Department of Teaching Media, University of Southampton (1983a)

Robinson, Brent, 'PROLOG to the Computer Tales' (1983b). Unpublished, but obtainable from the author at the Department of Education, University of Cambridge.

Robinson, Brent, 'Tomorrow, and Tomorrow, and Tomorrow . . .' in *English in Education* 18, 1, Spring 1984, pp. 47–53

Rubin, Andee, 'The Computer Confronts Language Arts: Cans and Shoulds for Education' in A. C. Wilkinson (ed.) *Classroom Computers and Cognitive Science* (Academic Press, New York, 1983)

Schwartz, Mimi, 'Computers and the Teaching of Writing' in *Educational Technology*, November 1982, pp. 27–29

Sharples, Mike, 'A Computer-Based Writing Scheme for Creative Writing' in R. Lewis and D. Tagg (eds.), *Computers and Education*, North-Holland Publishing Co. (1981a), pp. 483–88

Sharples, Mike, 'Microcomputers and Creative Writing' in J. A. M. Howe and P. M. Ross (eds.) *Microcomputers in Secondary Education: Issues and Techniques* (Kogan Page, 1981b), pp. 138–56

Sharples, Mike, 'Patterns of Words' (1984). Unpublished, but to appear in *Personal Computer World*.

Sharples, Mike, 'The Dynabook' (1984). Lecture given at the Micros and English Commission at the 1983 NATE conference (University of Surrey) and distributed at the International Commission on Computers and Literacy, University of Durham, England, April 1984. Now published as a research report by the Department of Artificial Intelligence, University of Edinburgh

Smith, Frank, 'Demonstrations, Engagement and Sensitivity: The choice between people and programs' in *Language Arts*, 58, 6, September 1981, pp. 634–42

Suttles, A. L., 'Computers and Writing: Contemporary Research and Innovative Programs' in *Computers, Reading and Language Arts* 1, 1, Summer 1983, pp. 33–37

Terrell, C. D. and O. Linyard, 'Evaluation of Electronic Learning Aids: Texas Instruments' SPEAK AND SPELL' in *International Journal of Man-Machine Studies*, 17 (1982), pp. 59–67

Wall, Shavaun M. and Nancy Taylor, 'Using Interactive Computer Programs in Teaching Higher Conceptual Skills: An Approach to Instruction in Writing' in *Educational Technology*, 22, February 1982, pp. 13–17

Wresch, William, 'Computers in English Class: Finally Beyond Grammar and Drills' in *College English*, 44, 5, September 1982, pp. 483–90

Zacchei, David, 'The Adventures and Exploits of the Dynamic STORYMAKER and TEXTMAN' in *Classroom Computer News*, May/June 1982, pp. 28–76

C   Journals and newsletters

CALLboard, ed. Graham Davies, Ealing College of Higher Education, St Mary's Road, London, W5 5RF

Computers in the Teaching of English (CITE), ed. Phil Moore, 25 King Edward Street, New Bradwell, Milton Keynes, Buckinghamshire, MK13 0BG

Computers, Reading and Language Arts, P.O. Box 13247, Oakland, California 94661, USA

Research in Word Processing Newsletter, Liberal Arts Department, South Dakota School of Mines and Technology, Rapid City, South Dakota 57701, USA

Appendix 2
Software Shortlist

ABC

Designers: David Butler and Daniel Chandler
Versions: BBC Model B (cassette/disc)
Source: Acornsoft
Description: A 'learner's screen-writer'. An introductory word-processing tool for young writers.

ADD–VERSE

Designer: Brent Robinson
Version: BBC Model B (cassette)
Source: CLASS
Description: A tool for creating and displaying kinetic poetry.

ADVENTURE

Designer: Unknown
Versions: RML 380Z (disc)
Source: Software Production Associates
Description: One of many text-only adventure games which are ideal for group discussion and as a focus for a variety of language workshop activities.

ADVENTURER

Designer: Daniel Chandler
Versions: BBC Model B (disc),
RML 380Z (disc)
Source: STORYMAKER version from Chelsea College
Description: A suite of software which allows users to create their own text-only adventure games.

ANIMAL

Designer: Adrian Jones
Version: BBC Model B (cassette)
Source: Tecmedia on behalf of MEP as part of Micro-Primer Pack no. 1
Description: One of many versions of a famous computer game in which the computer tries to 'guess' which animal the players are thinking of. If it fails to guess it, the users have to 'teach' the computer, by telling it which animal they had been thinking of, and, more importantly, typing a yes/no question which it will help it to guess correctly next time. Many versions exist, and any competent programmer could use the version in David Ahl's *BASIC Computer Games* (Workman Publishing, New York, 1978, p. 4–5) as a basis for implementing it on any microcomputer.

BANK STREET SPELLER

Designers: Bank Street College of Education
Versions: Apple II+ or Apple II (disc)
Source: Scholastic Publications Ltd
Description: A spelling checker for the BANK STREET WRITER (see below).

BANK STREET WRITER

Designers: Intentional Educations Inc., Franklin E. Smith and Bank Street College of Education
Versions: Apple II+ or II (48K) (disc), Atari (disc)
Source: Scholastic Publications Ltd
Description: A word-processor developed for young writers at Bank Street College of Education in New York. There are also packs of support materials.

CLASS WRITER and CLASS READERS

Designers: Trevor Medhurst and Brent Robinson
Versions: BBC Model B (cassette and disc)
Source: CLASS
Description: The Readers are a suite of programs which can all operate on text generated using the Writer. Reader 1 is OUTCOME, a variant on DEVELOPING TRAY (see below).

CLUES

Designers: Graham Field, Rosemary Fraser, Jan Stewart, David Towers (ITMA Collaboration)
Versions: BBC Model B, RML 380Z and 480Z
Source: Longman Micro Software (from the ITMA *Micros in the Primary Classroom* package, Module 3)
Description: A tool for masking and highlighting text in a variety of ways, including cloze procedure (though non-interactive and non-judgemental).

COMPUPOEM

Designer: Stephen Marcus
Version: Apple (disc)
Source: Stephen Marcus
Description: A playful and supportive introduction to writing one's own poetry, with the computer providing an initial framework.

DECODE

Designer: Richard Phillips
Version: RML 380Z
Source: Shell Centre for Mathematical Education
Description: A program in which the computer acts as an aid in decoding substitution ciphers.

DEVELOPING TRAY (also called simply TRAY)

Designer: Bob Moy
Versions: BBC Model B (cassette/disc), Electron (cassette),

RML 380Z (disc), Sinclair
Spectrum (cassette)
Source: Acornsoft, CLASS
(version called OUTCOME),
ILECC, Tecmedia (on behalf
of MEP)
Description: A game based on cloze
procedure in which readers
adopt predictive strategies in
order to uncover a text in which
all but the punctuation marks
have been masked out.

EDFAX

Designer: James Young
Version: BBC Model B (Disc)
Source: Tecmedia Limited (on
behalf of MEP)
Description: A 'teletext emulator' –
a microcomputer-based
version of an information
display and retrieval system
such as Ceefax or Oracle.
Allows users to store and
display pages of text and
graphics (including simple
animation). Useful for creating
an electronic newspaper,
bulletin-board or writing
workshop environment.

EDWORD

Designer: Peter Weston
Version: BBC Model B (ROM
chip)
Source: Clwyd Technics Ltd
Description: A word-processor
chip for use in schools,
designed as an introduction to
office word-processing.

FACEMAKER

Designer: Gloria Callaway
Version: BBC Model B

Source: ASK
Description: A prompt-driven
game in which the user can
create a variety of faces on the
screen from built-in parts.

FACTFILE and PICFILE

Designers: Daniel Chandler and
Anita Straker
Versions: BBC Model B (cassette),
Apple II (disc)
Source: Cambridge University
Press
Description: A simple introduction
to using one type of
information handling system.
The screen displays are clear
and readable. PICFILE draws
graphs.

GRAM

Designer: Mike Sharples
Version: BBC Model B (disc)
Source: Micros in Schools
Description: A tool allowing the
user to type in text and then
perform a variety of
grammatical transformations
on it.

THE HOBBIT

Designers: Philip Mitchell,
Veronica Megler, Alfred
Milgrom and Stuart Ritchie
Versions: BBC Model B (cassette),
Commodore 64 (cassette),
Sinclair Spectrum (cassette)
Source: Melbourne House
Description: An adventure game
based on Tolkien's story, of
which a copy is provided. The
BBC version is a text-only
game.

INFORM

Designers: Nottingham LEA
Version: BBC Model B
Source: Nottingham Computer
    Centre
Description: A simple data-
    handling system.

MARY ROSE

Designers: Ian Whitington and
    Barry Holmes
Version: BBC Model B (cassette)
Source: Ginn
Description: A computer-managed
    archaeological simulation.

MICROQUERY

Designer: AUCBE
Version: RML 380Z (disc)
Source: AUCBE
Description: A sophistcated
    information handling system,
    driven with a 'query language'.

MILLIKEN WORD-
PROCESSOR

Designers: Irene and Owen
    Thomas
Versions: Apple II/IIe
Source: Milliken
Description: A word-processing
    package for young learners,
    including a spelling checker
    and a thesaurus facility.

NEWSDESK

Designer: Patrick Scott
Version: Sinclair Spectrum
    (cassette)

Source: CLASS
Description: A computer-managed
    simulation game in which the
    players take on the roles of
    newspaper sub-editors. The
    computer acts as a teleprinter
    and offers screen-editing
    facilities.

NOMAN'S LAND

Designers: Don Clark and Daniel
    Chandler
Versions: Acorn Electron, BBC
    Model B (cassette/disc)
Source: Acornsoft
Description: A version of the
    famous decision-making game,
    EMPIRE (or
    HAMMURABI). Normally
    such games involve ruling a
    country and acquiring further
    territories by military might.
    Here the players are all
    members of a society and they
    must decide for themselves
    what their objectives are. They
    can also tailor much of the
    pattern of the game to their
    own preferences.

NOW PRESS RETURN

Designer: Roger McGough
Version: BBC Model B (cassette)
Source: BBC Soft (from the
    'Welcome' cassette)
Description: An amusing example
    of poetry which explores the
    interactive possibilities of the
    computer.

OTHER WORLDS

Designers: Tony Gray and Carl
    Billson
Versions: BBC Model B (cassette/
    disc)

Source: Ladybird-Longman
Micro Software
Description: Two programs, THE
EXPLORER and THE
INHABITANT, which
prompt the user to imagine and
describe a place from the point
of view of both an explorer and
an inhabitant.

PHILOSOPHER'S QUEST

Designer: Peter Kilworth
Version: BBC Model B (cassette)
Source: Acornsoft
Description: A text-only adventure
game.

PRIMARY PEN

Designers: GED Software
Version: BBC Model B
Source: GED Software
Description: A simple word-
processing program designed
for use at the primary level.

QUILL

Designers: Bertram Bruce and
Andee Rubin
Versions: Apple II+ (dual disc)
Source: D. C. Heath & Co.
Description: A writing environment
with text editor, 'planner',
message system and text
retrieval facility.

READING KLOOZ

Designer: Unknown
Versions: Apple II/IIe
Source: Midwest Publications
Description: A version of the
DEVELOPING TRAY
concept (q.v.).

SEEK

Designer: Jon Coupland
Versions: BBC Model B (cassette/
disc), RML 380Z (disc)
Source: Longman Micro Software
(part of the ITMA
Collaboration's *Micros in the
Primary Classroom* pack)
Description: A prompt-driven
information handling system,
based on a binary tree which is
graphically illustrated.

SPACE PROGRAMME
ALPHA

Designers: Joan Ashton and Ros
Butler
Version: BBC Model B (cassette)
Source: CLASS
Description: A package including a
computer-managed simulation
game and print materials. It is
intended to form the basis for a
half-term unit and involves a
variety of group activities.

SPACE RESCUE

Designers: Gill Barnes and Jenny
Perry
Versions: BBC Model B (cassette
and disc)
Source: CLASS
Description: A computer-managed
simulation game with print
materials intended to form the
basis of group activities in the
classroom.

SPELLCHECK

Designer: Beebugsoft
Versions: BBC Model B (disc) for
VIEW or WORDWISE
Source: Beebugsoft

Description: An automatic spelling checker for either of the two main ROM-based word-processors for the BBC Micro: VIEW or WORDWISE (see below). It may be used with single or dual drives and the maximum capacity is 15 000 words on a 100 K disc.

STORYMAKER

Designer: Daniel Chandler
Version: BBC Model B (listing)
Source: Educational Computing, November 1982, pp. 24–25
Description: A simple generator of bizarre situations which might form the basis for role-play and/or a story.

TALKBACK

Designers: David Butler and Daniel Chandler
Versions: Acorn Electron (cassette), BBC Model B (cassette/disc)
Source: Acornsoft
Description: A version of a famous program called ELIZA, which allowed the computer to simulate a Rogerian psychotherapist whilst the user typed in comments as a 'patient'. This version allows the user to create her own bank of match-words and responses. It also allows her to make one computer 'personality' have a dialogue with another. The 'script' may be printed out.

TERRIBLE TALES

Designers: Tony Gray and Carl Billson

Versions: BBC B (cassette/disc)
Source: Ladybird-Longman Micro Software
Description: Tales of monsters and giants are used to prompt the user to create her own.

TEXT DECODER

Designer: Daniel Chandler
Versions: BBC Model B (cassette/disc)
Source: MUSE
Description: A program which will turn a typed-in text into a simple substitution cipher, and will then act as an aid in allowing other users to decode it.

TEXT GRADER

Designers: John Mahoney and Peter Meiklejohn
Versions: BBC Model B (cassette/disc); RML 380Z and 480Z (disc)
Source: Hutchinson Software
Description: Users type in short texts, and then the program applies a variety of readability measures to them.

TREE OF KNOWLEDGE

Designer: Mike Biscoe-Taylor
Versions: Acorn Electron cassette, BBC Model B (cassette)
Source: Acornsoft
Description: This is a simple, prompt-driven information-handling system based on a binary tree, which is graphically illustrated. It can also be used to play the ANIMAL game.

THE UNORTHODOX ENGINEERS: THE PEN AND THE DARK

Designer: Keith Campbell
Versions: BBC Model B (cassette), Sinclair Spectrum
Source: Mosaic Publishing Ltd
Description: A text-only adventure game based on a science fiction short story by Colin Kapp, a copy of which is provided. An example of what British publishers are calling 'bookware'.

VIEW

Designer: Protechnic
Version: BBC Model B (ROM chip)
Source: Acornsoft
Description: A chip which turns the BBC Computer into a sophisticated word-processor.

WILT

Designer: Colin Harrison
Version: BBC Model B (cassette)
Source: Longman
Description: The 'hangman' game with a flower which wilts instead of the usual gruesome presentation. It includes a fascinating aid, in the form of frequency graphs for preceding and following letters in English words.

WORD–DANCE

Designers: David Butler and Daniel Chandler
Versions: BBC Model B (cassette/disc)
Source: CLASS

Description: A tool for creating and displaying kinetic text.

WORDHOARD

Designer: George Keith
Version: BBC Model B (disc)
Source: Cheshire Language Centre
Description: A computer-based thesaurus for young users.

WORD STORE/SYNONYMS

Designer: C. B. Pointeer
Version: BBC Model B (Disc)
Source: MUSE Software Library
Description: Two programs allowing users to create computer-based word-banks for personal or group use. There is space for 40 keywords, each with 20 associated words, so a single disc can handle 800 words. Large-size display type allows group viewing.

WORDWISE

Designer: Unknown
Version: BBC Model B (ROM chip)
Source: Computer Concepts
Description: A word-processor chip which is easy to use but which lacks the sophistication of VIEW (see above).

WRITE

Designer: Oxfordshire LEA
Versions: RML 380Z and 480Z
Source: David Walton
Description: A simple, easy-to-use word-processing program with 'Help' pages.

Software Suppliers

Acornsoft, Betjeman House,
104 Hills Road, Cambridge,
CB2 1LQ

Applied Systems Knowledge
(ASK), London House,
68 Upper Richmond Road,
London, SW15

Advisory Unit for Computer-
Based Education (AUCBE),
Endymion Road, Hatfield,
Hertfordshire, AL10 8AU

BBC Soft, BBC Publications,
The British Broadcasting
Corporation, 35 Marylebone
High Street, London,
W1M 4AA

Beebugsoft Ltd., P.O. Box 109,
High Wycombe, Bucks

Cambridge Language Arts
Software Services (CLASS),
93 Bedwardine Road, London,
SE19 3AY

Cambridge University Press, The
Edinburgh Building,
Shaftesbury Road, Cambridge,
CB2 2RU

Cheshire Language Centre,
North Cheshire College,
Fearnhead, Warrington,
Cheshire

Clwyd Technics Ltd., Coach
House, Kelsterton Road, Flint,
Clwyd, Wales

Computer Concepts, 16 Wayside,
Chipperfield, Hertfordshire

Educational Computing Section,
Chelsea College, University of
London, 552 Kings Road,
London, SW10 0UA

GED Software, 70 Stoke Road,
Bletchley, Milton Keynes,
Bucks

Ginn and Co. Ltd., Prebendal
House, Parson's Fee,
Aylesbury, Bucks, HP20 2QZ

D. C. Heath & Co., Electronic
Publishing Division, 125
Spring Street, Lexington,
Massachusetts 02173

Hutchinson Educational Ltd.,
17–21 Conway Street,
London, W1P 6JD

ILEA Educational Computer
Centre (ILECC), John Ruskin
Street, London, SE5 0PQ

Ladybird-Longman Micro
Software, Longman Group
Resources Unit, 33–35 Tanner
Row, York, YO1 1JP

Longman Micro Software,
Longman House, Burnt Mill,
Harlow, Essex

Stephen Marcus, Associate
Director, South Coast Writing
Project, Graduate School of
Education, University of
California, Santa Barbara,
California 93106

Melbourne House, Church Yard,
Tring, Hertfordshire,
HP25 5LU

Micros in Schools, The Open
University, Walton Hall,
Milton Keynes, Bucks,
MK7 6AA

Midwest Publications, Dept. 69,
P.O. Box 448, Pacific Grove,
California 93950

Mosaic Publishing Ltd.,
187 Upper Street, London,
N1 1RQ

MUSE Software Library,
FREEPOST, Bromsgrove,
B61 7BR (membership of
MUSE necessary)

Nottingham Computer Centre,
Eaton Hall, Retford,
Nottingham, DN22 0PR

Scholastic Publications Ltd.,
9 Parade, Leamington Spa,
Warwickshire, CV32 4DG

Shell Centre for Mathematical
Education, University Park,

Nottingham, NG7 2RD
Software Production Associates,
   P.O. Box 59,
   Royal Leamington Spa,
   Warwickshire, CV31 3QA
Tecmedia, 5 Granby Street,
   Loughborough,
   Leicestershire, LE11 3DU
David Walton, Computer
   Education Centre, Oxford
   LEA, Macclesfield House,
   New Road, Oxford, OX1 1NA

Appendix 3
Acornsoft Home
Education Guidelines

Acornsoft Home Education Authors' and Programmers' Guidelines
(August 1984, V4)
This appendix consists of an extract from guidelines produced by
Acornsoft, a leading publisher of software for the BBC and Electron
computers. It may serve to illustrate the responsible educational
philosophy and programming standards of their Home Education range.

These notes should be taken as a guide only. However, designers and
programmers are requested to consider all of these recommendations.

Type of program

- The program should be enjoyable to use for as wide an age/ability
  range as possible and it should be sufficiently flexible and interesting
  to encourage repeated use.
- The program should not purport to 'teach' or place an adult in a
  teacher's role.
- The development of learning strategies, the enjoyment of learning and
  the awareness (and reality) of control should be given a higher priority
  than learning specific skills or information.
- The programs should not be biased towards either sex.
- As a Home Education Section we are keen to avoid activities that have
  right or wrong solutions – life is seldom that simple. Consequently we
  dislike 'correct' and 'wrong' messages, smiling and frowning faces,
  pleasant tunes and unpleasant sounds or other forms of reward/
  punishment. The reward should be an intrinsic part of the subject, or
  main activity, of the program. Negative reinforcement has nothing to
  do with home education.
- There should be no tests, no test-makers, no arcade games, no
  illustrated lectures and no structured learning in the Home Education
  range. The use of scores should be kept to a minimum but, if
  necessary, 'points' rather than 'marks' should be used.

- The program should not use 'I' unless the simulation of a thinking being is essential to its purpose.
- The programs should make maximum use of the facilities provided by the BBC and Electron computers.

Movement through program

- We may wish to use the standard Acornsoft title page for both cassettes and discs.
- There should be a sound on/off option – Q for quiet and S for sound or a volume option.
- There should be a speech on/off option if speech is used.
- BREAK should not be protected. ESCAPE should return to a main menu/title page.
- Explanations of options are not a necessary part of the main menu.
- Home Education programs should be crash-proof and bug-free. An error trapping routine should always be included as a safeguard.

Length of program

- Packages should contain long program(s) rather than a series of short programs. Most Home Education programs should include information, decoration, music, speech, examples etc. and as many of the package options as possible – so that cassette users can avoid loading from tape and so that options can be selected in any order.
- The program must be able to load at PAGE &1B00 (for machines containing an Econet NFS): it can be moved down in memory to PAGE &E00 before it is run. Page D (addresses &D00–&DFF) should never be used, again in consideration of machines containing an Econet NFS.
- The program should be compressed to save tape space and tape-loading time.

Machine compatibility

The programs should run on the following:

- BBC Model B Basic I and Basic II, OS 1.2 with cassette and disc filing systems (programs that use files should offer a choice of filing systems).
- The Electron (preferably without requiring modifications to cater for loss of speed, sound channels and MODE 7)
- Colour TV, black and white TV, colour monitor, monochrome monitor
- A selection of popular printer makes (Epson, Olivetti, Ricoh, etc.)
- Acorn joysticks, etc.

Screen presentation

- Important diagrams, pictograms, text, etc. should contrast with the background colour to be clearly visible. (Some program users may be unable to discriminate between red and green.)
- The *TV command should not be used within programs. Instead programs should leave either the top or bottom line of the screen (or both lines) unused. The top line should not be used in programs that may be run on the Electron.
- Screens should not seem crowded or be a 'riot of colour'.

Text

- Text should be left-justified or centred or left-and-right justified. Normally there will be a border or space on either side of the text.
- Inexperienced readers should not be expected to read flashing text.
- Punctuation should be consistent and correctly used. Open punctuation is preferable. Capitals should be used to begin sentences and messages, for titles and particular labels and the names of keys. If a program is considered suitable for young children then all text should, as far as possible, cater for those who are still learning to read or be replaced by pictograms.
- Some documentation should be provided to accompany each program, preferably as a VIEW file. This may be a combination of notes on the use of the program, its educational value and applications, a description of the program and/or a guide through the program.
- All the information needed to use the program should, in addition to the documentation, be supplied as a part of the program itself – on a title page or a 'help' page – and be accessible at any time that the program is running.
- Program users should be referred to as the 'user' or the 'player'. There should be no discrimination between age or ability groups, though levels of difficulty may be selected.
- The term 'information' should be used in preference to 'instructions'.
- Spellings: 'to program' or 'a computer program', 'programmer', 'programming', etc. Disc rather than disk. SPACE BAR not SPACE-BAR.

Inputs and Prompts

- These should appear consistently throughout the program.
- If a keyboard response is expected this should be indicated by a message or symbol on the screen.
- The message 'Press SPACE BAR to continue', with the flashing cursor immediately to its right, is usual before a screen change.

- The flashing cursor should appear to the right of (or occasionally below) all prompts.
- Inputs should be limited to an appropriate field length (i.e. 3 for Yes/No responses).
- DELETE and RETURN should normally be used to correct and complete inputs and it may be necessary to indicate when these keys should be used.
- Flush the keyboard buffer before accepting inputs (*FX15 does this for OSO.1).
- The program should react immediately when a key is pressed.
- Inputs should respond correctly regardless of whether SHIFT LOCK or CAPS LOCK is on or not. For example Y/N prompts should accept any one of the characters YyNn, and ! " # % $ & ' ( ) should be accepted as 1 2 3 4 5 6 7 8 9.
- Text inputs should normally accept both upper and lower case.

Appendix 4
A Guide to the Jargon

adventure game: a type of game originally developed on mainframe computers but now available as home entertainment software for most microcomputers. The players find themselves in environments which they 'explore' by typing in simple sentences that tell the computer what direction they want to go, what objects they want to pick up or examine, etc.

AI: see 'artificial intelligence'

artificial intelligence (AI): quasi-intelligent behaviour exhibited by computers or robots. The term is used to describe systems which can be made to emulate aspects of human thinking processes such as reasoning, learning and self-correction. Also used to refer to the field of research concerned with developing and studying such systems.

authoring language: a high-level programming language which enables those unskilled in writing programs in conventional programming languages (such as BASIC) to write a special-purpose program (for example, for computer-assisted instruction).

authoring system: software which prompts the user to provide data and then creates a special-purpose tool which will function as a program.

BASIC: a simple (though rather primitive) high-level programming language using recognizable English words. Most microcomputers have BASIC built-in. Different 'dialects' are used for different types of computers, but programs written in a fairly standard subset of BASIC are not difficult to convert for a particular type of computer.

bookware: a term which British publishers are beginning to use to describe software closely associated with, and usually sold together with, a printed book (most commonly narrative fiction).

branch: part of a computer program or information retrieval system in which a choice is made between alternative routes through the sequence of frames or events.

bug: a flaw in a program resulting mainly from mistyping, inadequate thinking through of the logic of the program or misunderstanding of some aspect of the programming language being used. See also 'debugging'

CAI: see 'computer-assisted instruction'

CAL: see 'computer-assisted learning'

CAL package (UK): a multi-media collection of learning materials on a specific topic, including one or more computer programs.

CBE, CBL: computer-based education/learning – a synonym for computer-assisted instruction.

character: a symbol – for example, a letter, a number or a punctuation mark. Note: spaces between words also count as characters.

character set: (a) a full set of keyboard characters which a particular computer system can display on the screen. Some systems offer a range of complete character sets, in different sizes and styles. They do not necessarily correspond with (b) the full set of keyboard characters which a particular computer printer can print out. With daisy-wheel printers (q.v.) these are provided as type-faces on the detachable daisy-wheels themselves. With dot-matrix printers (q.v.) a more limited range of sizes and styles may be generated from the computer.

cloze software: software based in some sense on the technique of cloze procedure used by reading teachers. Note that whereas for many teachers the essence of this technique would be to ask students to suggest words which might fit into the context of a passage from which they had been deliberately deleted, any cloze software which attempts to make judgements on the suitability of any substitutions inevitably narrows the activity into the guessing of 'correct' answers.

CMI, CML: see 'computer-managed learning'

command language: a limited set of commands (and the syntax governing their use) which is used as the basis for the 'drive system' (q.v.) in some programs. It is a system used particularly in 'relational databases' (q.v.)

computer: a fast, general-purpose electronic device for storing and manipulating symbols.

computer-assisted (or aided) instruction (CAI): the use of computers to provide instruction or drill-and-practice. Widely used in the US to include what in the UK is referred to as CAL.

computer-assisted (or aided) learning (CAL): the use of the computer to provide learning opportunities.

computer awareness: a term frequently used to describe an awareness of the uses and implications of the use of computers in general (not specifically in education).

computer literacy: a term often used loosely to refer to an ability to operate computers (sometimes also including programming and/or computer awareness). Perhaps more usefully used to refer to new dimensions of traditional literacy required by the computer medium, such as in screen-reading, writing with a word-processor and information retrieval.

computer-managed learning, CML (UK) and *computer-managed instruction, CMI (US):* the use of computers for monitoring, analysing and reporting on users' progress in individualized instruction.

computer system: a complete computer, including the CPU (often built into the keyboard), a VDU and backing store, as well as any other linked peripherals such as a printer.

content game: an educational game in which the main intention is for users to learn about the subject-matter dealt with. See also 'process game'

content-free software: software in which the subject-matter is chosen by users, who must enter the relevant data themselves.

courseware: in the UK this term is commonly used to mean educational materials associated with the computer software (often print materials). In the US the term more commonly refers to the educational software itself.

cpl: characters per line.

cps: characters per second. Used in referring to printer speed.

crash: a term used to refer to the condition when a program which is running comes to a premature halt, offering the user no obvious way of making it resume functioning.

crashproofing: a programmer's attempt to build safeguards into a program to ensure that users will not unwittingly crash it.

CRT: cathode-ray tube (as in a television or monitor). In the US, often used to mean VDU (see 'visual display unit').

cursor: a symbol (sometimes flashing) shown on the screen to indicate where the next typed character will appear. It can often be moved around the screen by means of up, down, left and right arrows.

daisy-wheel printer: a computer printer which produces a variety of good quality type because the plastic typeface 'wheels' are interchangeable. It is therefore widely used for commercial word-processing.

data: in computing, numbers, words or facts in a form suitable for storage in a computer.

database: an organized collection of computerized data which can be searched for specific information.

datafile: recorded data organized in a consistent format (for example, name, address, telephone number) for use by a program.

data-processing: sorting or reformulating quantities of data in some way, usually with computer-based systems.

debugging: removing flaws from a program.

dedicated: an adjective used to describe a piece of hardware designed for a specific application. For example, a dedicated word-processor is one which is built as a word-processor rather than a computer which can also run word-processing software.

DELETE: a named key on many micros which, when pressed, deletes on the VDU the previous character typed on the keyboard.

descriptor: in an information retrieval system (especially bibliographic systems) the key concepts associated with individual records in a file, allowing the user to retrieve a file without knowing its contents (for example, an article on peace education might have the descriptor 'peace' even though the title did not include the word).

dialect: in computing, a version of a particular programming language with some unique variations.

disc (also *disk* or *diskette*): see 'floppy disc'

disc-drive unit: a device which reads from floppy discs into a computer. The disc revolves at high speed, and data is transmitted to and from it through read/write heads.

documentation: the print materials associated with a computer system or a computer program. Documentation includes: the user manual for a particular computer (including technical information); program notes, listings, flow-charts and sample output. Sometimes in UK misleadingly used to include associated learning materials

dot-matrix printer: a computer printer which forms characters from tiny dots made by needles hitting a ribbon.

draft quality: refers to printing usually done by dot-matrix printers (q.v.), that is not 'letter quality' (q.v.). Some dot-matrix printers, however, produce printing close to letter quality (see 'near letter quality').

drivecharts: a term used by the UK ITMA project to refer to a diagram that summarizes the operation of a given program.

drive system: (also *front end, user interface*): the basic design which controls the way a program appears to operate, from the point of view of the user. Examples are: function-key driven (q.v.), menu-driven (q.v.), command language driven (q.v.).

Dynabook: 'a personal dynamic medium the size of a notebook . . . which could be owned by everyone and could have the power to handle virtually all of its owner's information-related needs' (Alan Kay and Adele Goldberg, 'Personal Dynamic Media' in *Computer*, 10, pp. 31–41, 1977).

editing facilities: computer functions which enable the user to make changes to text on the screen. The DELETE key is a simple editing facility.

educational computing: the use of computers for educational purposes as opposed to 'computer education' (the study of computers).

electronic blackboard: a term used to refer to a type of program used by a teacher to provide a visual display for large-group presentation.

electronic mail: the transmission of messages between computerized equipment, usually via the telephone line.

electronic publishing: writing on a computer and disseminating the writing via some kind of network of computers (usually via the telephone system) to other users of the network.

encoding: writing a computer program in the precise code of a programming language.

expert system: a program which uses the expert knowledge with which it has been provided to process solutions to formally-structured problems. For instance, an expert system might have been provided with specialist data and rules for answering questions on a topic such as plant identification.

field: in information retrieval, a defined part of a record in a datafile (for example, that which is set aside for a telephone number).

file: see 'datafile'

floppy disc: (also referred to as a *diskette*): a lightweight medium for the rapid storage and retrieval of programs and data. Rather like a small flimsy audio record. Coated with a magnetic material and enclosed in a square envelope within which it can revolve.

flow-chart: a diagram representing the sequence of steps in a program or a problem.

formatting (also *re-formatting*): in word-processing, a facility to tidy up the appearance of a text by removing unwanted gaps, and sometimes also justification (q.v.).

frame: the contents of the visual display screen at any one time.

friction feed: a capability which some computer printers have for accepting single sheets of typing paper (see also tractor feed).

front end: a term used to refer to the way a programming language or a program appears to operate, from the point of view of users. See also 'drive system'

fully-formed characters: refers to printing done with a full typeface, as opposed to a character formed by a dot-matrix printer (q.v.).

function-keys: keys set aside on some computer keyboards which can be assigned special functions for the purposes of a particular program (on the BBC Computer these are the red keys).

function-key driven program: a program in which most of the actions which it can perform are caused by the user pressing specific function keys (q.v.). See also 'drive system'

graphics: pictures and diagrams created on a computer (as opposed to text). See also 'high-resolution' and 'low-resolution graphics'

hands-on: using, rather than just talking about, computers.

hard-copy: printed computer output forming a durable record.

hardware: the physical units which constitute a computer system.

Hawthorne effect: usually refers to a tendency for the behaviour of the subjects of an experiment to be affected by the presence of observers. Sometimes used to mean simply a tendency for a technique (such as using computers) to work because of the novelty factor.

high-level language: a programming language closer to natural vocabulary than machine code.

high-resolution graphics: graphics capable of displaying fine lines.

home computer: see 'personal computer'

informatics: a term sometimes used to refer to the study of the way we manipulate information, and its social implications.

information: sometimes distinguished from data (which may not provide information) as data organized in some way which makes it meaningful.

information literacy: competence to cope with the efficient retrieval of data

– particularly using computerized databases.

information processing: see 'data-processing'

information retrieval: searching large quantities of data for that which meets specified criteria.

information technology (IT): the technology associated with the communication, storage and retrieval of data.

input: whatever is typed into a computer, whether raw data, a program, or a student's answer to a question.

insert mode: in word-processing, a system (usually an option) in which typing in the midst of existing text on the screen inserts each new letter into the text, 'pushing' the existing text letter-by-letter in front of it. See also 'overwrite mode'

interactive: in computing, usually used to refer to some kind of dialogue between computer and user. Misleading when applied to programs in which the user is simply prompted to answer 'yes' or 'no'.

interactive fiction: narratives displayed on the video screen of a computer, which allow the reader to intervene, either by choosing particular paths through a branching plot, or by entering dialogue or narrative of her own which may or may not cause such branching. See also 'adventure games'

invisible writing: an experimental writing technique in which children are encouraged to attempt some kinds of writing using empty ball-point pens on carbon paper, since studies have suggested that this may lead some writers to be less distracted from developing a line of thought by indulging in editing at too early a stage. Dr Stephen Marcus has advocated the use of this technique when writing with computers, by turning off the visual display or turning it away from the writer so that it can be viewed only by a partner.

IT: see 'information technology'

justification: in word-processing, a facility whereby text can be neatly aligned with one or both margins, removing the ragged edges of paragraphs and forming a 'solid' column.

keyboard: a set of keys forming part of a computer system which are similar to those of a typewriter. The user's main means of communicating with the computer.

keyword matching: the computer's identifying of the important words typed in by the user by matching them with a checklist stored in the computer program. A technique used in adventure games (q.v.), information retrieval (q.v.), and at a more sophisticated level, AI (q.v.).

kinetic text: text which moves. This is one use of the computer as a writing medium which allows users to explore dimensions of writing which it would be difficult, if not impossible, to accomplish with pen and paper.

language: see 'programming language'

legibility: applied to electronic text, this often neglected factor includes the clarity of the character set, the density of characters per line and lines per frame, colour contrast, birghtness and layout. A useful paper on the subject by Brent Robinson is listed in Appendix 1.

letter-quality printing: applied to the quality of type produced by some computer printers (usually daisy-wheel, q.v.). Comparable to the clear, rounded type produced by an electronic 'golfball' typewriter.

listing: a printed list of program instructions, usually produced by the computer printer.

listing paper (also *printout paper*)*:* paper for printing on a computer printer. Usually folded, perforated and with holes at the edges to be used by the printer's tractor feed mechanism (q.v.).

LOAD, loading: a command used to transfer the contents of a program from an audio cassette or floppy disc into internal memory (RAM).

locus of control: used in this book to refer to where on an imaginary spectrum the control of an activity resides – close to the user or close to the computer program. Derived from Dr Jim Levin.

Logo: a high-level programming language designed for children by Wallace Feurzeig and Seymour Papert. It is most well-known for its suitability for geometrical drawing, but full versions of the language have sophisticated capabilities for manipulating text (as the work of Mike Sharples in Britain has demonstrated).

low-level language: a programming language close to that used internally by the computer itself, such as assembly language.

low-resolution graphics: primitive graphics where the image displayed is made up of square blocks rather than fine dots.

machine: what computer people call the computer.

mainframe computer: a very large (traditional) computer installation which can have numerous terminals connected to it.

memory: a computer's store for data and programs. Usually used to refer to internal (immediate) memory – particularly RAM (but sometimes also ROM). Occasionally used to include external backing store memory, for example, audio-cassettes or floppy discs.

memory size: the size of available RAM (immediate memory) on a particular computer, usually expressed in units called 'K' (e.g. 32 K), where K is 1024. Only programs of this size or smaller can run on the computer.

menu: a part of a program shown on a VDU as a list of choices of action for the user. Each choice leads down a different branch of the program.

menu-driven program: a program in which the user can easily return to the menu (q.v.) to select an option.

microcomputer (sometimes simply *micro* in the UK): a small computer with a microprocessor (CPU) mounted on a board. Usually used to mean also the VDU and the backing store, although this might be more usefully described as a microcomputer system.

microworlds: a term used by advocates of the Logo programming language to mean a computer-based system for exploratory learning within a specified 'environment' such as 'turtle graphics'.

Microwriter: a British hand-held (battery-operated) word-processor with only six keys and a narrow LCD display. It can be plugged into a conventional monitor when a larger display is required and uses non-volatile memory.

mini-computer: a medium-size computer which is usually part of a larger system. Widely used in business applications.

monitor: a television-like video display for computer output. Also a computing term referring to a technical means of monitoring the computer's internal operation.

natural language: ordinary conversational language. In computing, a field in artificial intelligence research in which programs are developed to allow users to communicate with the computer (usually via the keyboard) in everyday language.

near-letter quality (NLQ): refers to the quality of text printed by a dot-matrix printer (q.v.) when it resembles that produced by an inked-ribbon typewriter.

network: any system consisting of a series of connected points. In computing, usually a system in which several computers are linked to each other or in which a number of terminals are connected to a computer.

neutrality of technology: the idea that we can separate tools from the interests which bring them into being and the use to which they are put.

OCR: optical character recognition. The direct reading of printed (and sometimes handwritten) text by a computer.

overwrite mode: in word-processing, a system (usually an option) in which typing on top of existing text on the screen replaces the former letters with those being typed 'over' them. See also 'insert mode'

paging: an approach to presenting electronic text by displaying a frame, clearing the screen, displaying another, and so on. This method is much closer to the act of turning a page than scrolling (q.v.).

Pascal: a structured high-level programming language.

PC: see 'personal computer'

peripherals: the input and output devices attached to the computer – for example, a VDU, an audio-cassette recorder and a printer.

personal computer (PC): a microcomputer system designed for, or widely used in, a domestic setting.

PILOT: a simple high-level programming language sometimes used for CAI. It is designed to allow teachers to write their own programs. It is particularly valued for the ease with which it can match a response with a series of alternatives provided by the program author.

printer: a device which can be connected to a computer to produce printed output.

printout: see 'hard-copy'

printout paper: see 'listing paper'

process games: educational games in which the main intention is for learners to acquire or extend particular learning strategies rather than their knowledge of the content.

program: a complete sequence of precise coded instructions for the computer to make it perform a particular task. The original is typed into a computer, although subsequent copies may be loaded from audio cassette or floppy disc. In British usage, not to be confused with programme (as in 'a television programme' or 'a programme of activities').

program design: the process of deciding what a program is intended to do and what the user should see and do at each stage.

program development: the process of designing, programming, debugging and validating a program.

programmed instruction: a teaching method for individual instruction in which a precisely-defined sequence of steps must be followed.

programmer: anyone who encodes computer programs.

programming language: a set of coded instructions, together with the necessary syntax, allowing the user to control the computer. A variety of languages exist (such as BASIC and Pascal), some of which were designed for specific purposes (LISP, for instance, was designed for artificial intelligence research).

program specification: the detailed list of requirements given to a programmer so that he or she knows exactly what the program must do.

PROLOG: a recent programming language which Richard Ennals and others in Britain have argued may be particularly suitable for teachers concerned with the Language Arts.

prompt: a character (often a question mark or a 'greater than' sign (>) displayed on the VDU screen, indicating that the computer is waiting for the user to type something. Sometimes used to include a brief text prompting the user.

QWERTY: refers to the conventional keyboard layout of most typewriters and computers.

readability software: programs that allow the user to enter short passages of text, after which the software applies to them one or more readability measures, and displays the results. Most commonly used by teachers for checking textbooks or teacher-produced resources. Such software will become far more widely used when cheap OCR units (q.v.) become available.

real time: a program is said to be operating in 'real time' if the passage of time recorded in a program has a recognizable relationship to the real passage of time.

response time: the average time taken for the computer to respond to a user's input. Sometimes used also to refer to the time taken for the user to respond to a prompt in a program.

routing: guiding the user through an appropriate sequence of frames in a program. See 'branch' and 'tree structure'

SAVE, saving: a command to the computer which is typed to transfer a program from the main memory to a backing store such as audio-cassette or floppy disc.

screen chart: a term sometimes used in the UK to describe a diagram consisting of a series of boxes containing text and graphics drawn up by a program designer to tell the programmer exactly what should appear on the screen at each stage in a program.

screen design: the choice of suitable layouts, colours, wording and graphics for individual frames within programs. Sometimes also used to refer to the sequencing of such frames as part of the process of program design. See also 'legibility'

screen-reading: reading electronic text. Efficient reading of such text may involve some quite different strategies from reading a printed page.

screen size: the number of lines and characters per line that a computer can display (several sizes are possible on many microcomputers).

scrolling: the phenomenon whereby, when a screen has been filled with the maximum number of lines for its screen size, each additional line of text causes the remainder of the text to rise up the screen by one line, and the previous top line vanishes from immediate view. As a way of presenting electronic text to a reader it contrasts with paging (q.v.).

SHIFT: one of the keys on the computer keyboard similar in function to that on a typewriter. It alters the range of characters generated by pressing the alphanumeric keys. For instance, pressing SHIFT may allow you to produce capital letters rather than lower-case letters.

simulation: in computing, exploring the effect of various strategies on pre-defined models of situations, or software comprising such models.

software: in computing, programs and data which are used to control the hardware.

software protection: any technique employed to prevent the unauthorized reproduction of a program.

specification: see 'program specification'

spelling checkers: programs (usually used in conjunction with word-processing packages) which can check all the words in a text against a built-in word-bank, and, when unrecognized words are discovered, can prompt the user either to add the word to the word-bank or to retype the word.

string: a character or a number of connected characters which, although it may contain numbers, is not to be used for calculation and is therefore treated by the computer as a sequence of alphabetical symbols.

tachistoscope software: programs which allow the computer to function as a tachistoscope, an instrument sometimes used with the intention of increasing the user's reading speed, enabling words to be flashed on the screen for exactly timed periods.

technology: all technical means and knowledge, the interests which control them and the uses to which they are put. Reading and writing (though not language) constitute a technology.

telecommunications: the transmission of data by telephone, television, cable, satellite etc., together with the technology and theory of such communications.

teletext: a simple computerized information system provided by broadcasting companies for users with the appropriate adaptor on their own television receivers. For example, Ceefax and Oracle in the UK.

tractor feed: a standard capability on computer printers which enables them to accept conventional computer printout or 'listing paper'. See also 'friction feed'

tree structure: a fundamental framework for structuring the sequence of choices in a program or retrieval system. Prestel is a good example, where the user may proceed from a general index through more specific branches to the particular frame required.

user-friendly: an adjective used to describe qualities in a program which makes it less remote from the individual user. It may include the use of a user's name on the screen, avoidance of computer jargon, ease of use and a gentle element of humour.

user group: a group of users of a particular computer – largely hobbyists.

user interface: see 'front end'

VDU: see 'visual display unit'

videodisc: a disc which can be used for storing and replaying video film via a television receiver, but which can also be used to store software. Since such software may also control access to both video and other software the 'interactive videodisc' can be a powerful and flexible educational resource.

video monitor: a visual display unit which may or may not be combined with a broadcast television receiver. Those specially designed as monitors produce a sharper picture when used with microcomputers.

videotex: (note spelling): sometimes used to include both viewdata and teletext, and sometimes used as a synonym for viewdata alone.

viewdata: a computerized information retrieval system which uses the telephone system to link users to a database, allowing them to select particular frames, or to choose and order information or goods. Prestel in Britain is one example; Telidon in Canada is another.

visual display unit (VDU): a video monitor or a television receiver used to display the user's input and the output from the computer.

word-processing, WP: editing, manipulating, storing and printing text on a dedicated word-processor or on a computer running a word-processing program.

word-processor: (a) a dedicated (special-purpose) computer designed at least primarily for word-processing; (b) a computer behaving as a word-processor because of the use of word-processing software (or firmware).

wraparound: a term used to refer to a built-in function in screen-writing systems which, whilst the user types, automatically moves words onto the next line if they would otherwise be split by the margin.

NOTE: Some of these definitions are drawn from the glossary in Daniel Chandler's book *Young Learners and the Microcomputer* (Open University Press, 1984).

Notes to the Text

Chapter 1   Computers and Literacy

1 See Walter Ong, *Orality and Literacy* (Methuen, 1982).
2 Harold Innis, *The Bias of Communication* (University of Toronto Press, 1951).
3 The term 'networked society' is used here to refer to a situation where the general public has easy, regular access to a large national and even international network of linked computers.
4 See Chandler (1984), p. 30.
5 Dr Mike Sharples suggests that low-level editing may simply be a consequence of the nature of current word-processors, and that improved systems may alter this phenomenon.
6 See the references to Peggy in Chandler (1984), pp. 29–31.
7 Samuel Butler, *Erewhon and Erewhon Revisited* (New York: Modern Library, 1927), p. 234.
8 F. R. Leavis and Denys Thompson, *Culture and Environment* (Chatto and Windus, 1950), p. 3.
9 Ibid., p. 2.
10 Ibid., p. 97.
11 William Morris, *News from Nowhere* (Longmans Green and Co., 1891), p. 113.
12 Jan Hawkins, Karen Sheingold, Maryl Gearhart and Chana Berger, *Microcomputers in Schools – Impact on the Social Life of Elementary Classrooms* (mimeo, Bank Street College, New York, 1982).
13 See Papert (1980).
14 Seymour Papert in a lecture in London on 4 September 1983.

Chapter 2   Young Writers and the Computer

1 For further descriptions of the use of Microwriters with children see Clark (1983), and High and Fox (1984).
2 Stephen Marcus gives his own accounts of COMPUPOEM in Marcus (1982a/b).
3 An introduction to invisible writing can be found in Marcus & Blau (1983).

Chapter 3   Electronic Text

1 A stimulating discussion of future directions, in particular Alan Kay's Dynabook concept, can be found in Sharples (1984).

2 For a fuller treatment of some of the issues in this chapter see Robinson (1983a).

Chapter 4 Talking, Listening and the Microcomputer
1 Lewis Knowles, *Encouraging Talk* (Methuen, 1983), p. 19.
2 See Oliver and Boyd's forthcoming *Now Hear This*.
3 Anthony Adams and John Pearce, *Every English Teacher* (Oxford University Press, 1974).
4 See Chandler (1982a).
5 See Sharples (1981b), and such programs as Chelsea College's forthcoming STORYMAKER.
6 The address of CLASS can be found in Appendix 2.
7 John Latham, quoted in MEP's *English Resource Pack* No. 1 (March 1984).
8 See Robinson (1983b).

Chapter 5 Evaluating Computer Programs
1 For the secondary English teacher a useful case-study by Patrick Scott appears in Chandler (1983).
2 At a British Department of Education and Science conference in January 1984 it was felt that there is a good case for schools having available different kinds of word-processor for different purposes [D.C.].
3 A formal checklist for evaluating software has been produced for language arts teachers by NCTE in the USA (see Appendix 1).

Chapter 6 Designing Software
1 Chandler (1984).
2 See Papert (1980).
3 Dr Irene Thomas in a personal communication with the author, October 1984.
4 Ibid.
5 Ibid.
6 An example of the responsible stance which commercial concerns could adopt is reflected in Acornsoft's guidelines for program proposals in their Home Education range, printed in Appendix 3.

Chapter 7 The Dangers of Computers in Literacy Education
1 See M. Nystrand, *Language as a Way of Knowing* (Toronto, OISE Press, 1977).
2 See, for example, Gordon Wells, *Learning Through Interaction* (Cambridge University Press, 1981).
3 See, for example: James Britton, *Language and Learning* (Penguin, 1970).

4 Paulo Freire, 'The Importance of the Act of Reading' in *Journal of Education* 165 (1983), pp. 5–11.

5 See K. S. Goodman, 'Reading as a Psycholinguistic Guessing Game' in *Journal of the Reading Specialist* 4 (1967), pp. 126–35, and Frank Smith, *Understanding Reading*, 2nd edn. (New York, Holt, Rinehart & Winston, 1978).

6 See T. Lê, 'Cognitive and Meditative Aspects of Reading' in *Language Arts* 61 (1984), pp. 351–55 and J. Moffett, 'Reading and Writing as Meditation' in *Language Arts* 60 (1983), pp. 315–20.

7 C. Edelsky and K. Smith, 'Is that Writing – Or Are Those Marks Just a Figment of Your Curriculum?' in *Language Arts* 61 (1984), pp. 24–32.

8 B. Fillion, 'Language Across the Curriculum' in *McGill Journal of Education* 14 (1979), pp. 47–60.

9 Education Commission of the States, *The Information Society: Are High School Graduates Ready?* (Denver, 1982).

10 M. Stubbs, *Language, Schools and Classrooms* (London, Methuen, 1976), p. 8.

11 See, for example: Douglas Barnes, *From Communication to Curriculum* (Penguin, 1970) and Stubbs, *Language, Schools and Classrooms*.

12 See, for example: Donald Graves, 'We Won't Let Them Write' in *Language Arts* 55 (1978), pp. 635–40.

13 David Dillon and Dennis Searle, 'The Message of Marking' in *Research in the Teaching of English* 14 (1980), pp. 233–42.

14 E. Lunzer and K. Gardner (eds.), '*The Effective Use of Reading* (London, Heinemann, 1980).

15 A. D. Edwards and V. Furlong, *The Language of Teaching: Meaning in Classroom Interaction* (London, Heinemann, 1978).

16 Barnes, *From Communication to Curriculum*.

17 Lunzer and Gardner, *The Effective Use of Reading*.

18 L. Vygotsky, *Thought and Language* (Cambridge, Mass., MIT Press, 1962).

19 Dennis Searle, 'Two Contexts for Adolescent Language: Classroom Learning and the Discussion of Extra-School Experience' (Unpublished PhD thesis, University of London, 1981).

20 William Labov, 'The Logic of Nonstandard English' in J. Alatis (ed.), *Linguistics and the Teaching of English to Speakers of Other Languages*, Georgetown Monographs on Language and Linguistics, vol. 22 (Washington D.C., Georgetown University Press, 1969).

21 Maya Angelou, *I Know Why the Caged Bird Sings* (New York, Bantam, 1971), p. 78.

22 Ibid., p. 869.

23 Margaret Meek, *Learning to Read* (London, Bodley Head, 1982) and *Achieving Literacy* (London, Routledge and Kegan Paul, 1983).

24 C. F. Kaestle, 'Perspectives: Literacy and Mainstream Culture in American History' in *Language Arts* 58 (1981), pp. 207–218.

25 Paulo Freire, *Pedagogy of the Oppressed* (New York, Seabury Press, 1970).

26 M. Fetler, *Computer Literacy of California High School Seniors* (Educational Data Center, California Department of Education, Sacramento, 1983).

27 J. Anyon, 'Social Class and the Hidden Curriculum of Work' in *Journal of Education* 162 (1980), pp. 67–92.

28 Ibid., p. 73.

29 Center for the Social Organization of Schools, *School Uses of Microcomputers: Reports from a National Survey* (Baltimore, John Hopkins University, 1983).

30 R. Jones, D. Porter and R. Rubis, *A Survey of the Use of Microcomputers in British Columbia Schools* (Burnaby, B. C., Simon Fraser University, 1983).

31 C.S.O.S., *School Uses of Microcomputers*.

32 'Warnings About Classroom Computers' in *Macleans*, August 13, 1984, p. 49.

33 L. Rosenblatt, *The Reader, the Text and the Poem* (Southern Illinois University Press, 1978).

34 B. Bruce, S. Michaels and K. Watson-Gegeo, 'Reviewing the Black History Show' in *Language Arts* (in press).

35 Jean-Paul Sartre, 'Words' in A. Melnick and J. Merritt (eds.), *Reading Today and Tomorrow* (London, University of London Press, 1972), p. 193.

36 Richard Rodriguez, *Hunger of Memory* (Boston, Godine, 1981), p. 62.

37 M. Polanyi, *Meaning* (University of Chicago Press, 1959), p. 10.

38 Robert Frost, 'The Road Not Taken' in E. C. Latham (ed.), *The Poetry of Robert Frost* (New York, Holt, Rinehart & Winston, 1969).

Chapter 8   The Future of Literacy

1 John Naisbitt, *Megatrends* (Warner Books, 1982).

2 The Delphi Method is an approach to opinion polling which uses feedback from respondents to reach some kind of consensus. Both of the editors are involved in Barber and LaConte's study.

3 William Miller in an address to the Modern Language Association, New York, 1983.

Index of Names

Programs

Note: Programs in Appendix 2 are asterisked.

Index of Topics